El Narcotraficante

*Inter-America Series / Edited by Duncan Earle,
Howard Campbell, and John Peterson*

In the new "Inter-American" epoch to come, our borderland
zones may expand well past the confines of geopolitical lines.
Social knowledge of these dynamic interfaces offers rich insights
into the pressing and complex issues that affect both the
borderlands and beyond. The Inter-America Series comprises a
wide interdisciplinary range of cutting-edge books that explicitly
or implicitly enlist border issues to discuss larger concepts,
perspectives, and theories from the "borderland" vantage and will
be appropriate for the classroom, the library, and the wider
reading public.

EL NARCOTRAFICANTE
Narcocorridos and the Construction of a Cultural Persona on the U.S.-Mexico Border

Mark Cameron Edberg
Foreword by Howard Campbell

 University of Texas Press, Austin

Tape and CD covers used by permission of Cintas Acuario
International

First edition, 2004

Requests for permission to reproduce material from this
work should be sent to Permissions, University of Texas Press,
P.O. Box 7819, Austin, TX 78713-7819.

⊗ The paper used in this book meets the minimum
requirements of ANSI/NISO Z39.48-1992 (R1997) (permanence
of paper).

Library of Congress Cataloging-in-Publication Data

Edberg, Mark Cameron, 1955–
El narcotraficante : narcocorridos and the construction of a
cultural persona on the U.S.-Mexico border / Mark Cameron
Edberg ; foreword by Howard Campbell.
    p.   cm. — (Inter-America series)
Includes bibliographical references and index.
ISBN 0-292-70182-9 (cloth : alk. paper)—
ISBN 0-292-70206-x (pbk. : alk. paper)
1. Drug traffic—Mexico.   2. Drug traffic—Mexico—Folklore.
3. Drug traffic—Mexico—Songs and music.   4. Narcotics
dealers—Mexico—Folklore.   5. Narcotics dealers—Mexico—
Songs and music.   6. Drugs in popular music.   7. Corridos—
Mexico.   8. Mexican Americans in popular culture.
9. Mexico—Social life and customs.   I. Title.   II. Series.
HV5840.M6E33 2004
306′.1—dc22
2003025802

Contents

Illustrations

Foreword

Howard Campbell

It's six o'clock on a weekday evening in Ciudad Juárez, Chihua-hua, Mexico. Radios in the colonias, barrios, and cantinas are tuned to XEPZ 1190, Radio Norteña. A familiar jingle wafts over the airwaves; it's "Hour of the Corridos," with "el Abuelo Chabelo" (Grandfather Chabelo, a playful inversion of a popular Mexican tele-vision character, Chabelo, an adult dressed in children's clothing who is the star of one of the main children's programs). The phones start ringing. The first caller, a child, wants to hear "El Gato de Chihuahua" (The Cat from Chihuahua). El Abuelo asks the child to solve a riddle and then plays her song. The next caller, a woman, wants to hear "Camelia la Tejana" (Camelia, the Texan). El Abuelo agrees to her request, then scandalously flirts with her (el Abuelo is eighty-five years old and badly wrinkled). He concludes the con-versation with an off-color joke, to the delight of the caller, and a goofy laugh track in the background. To another caller: "Which co-rrido do you want to hear? OK, 'Jefe de Jefes' (Boss of the Bosses)." Another joke and then el Abuelo switches to one of his alter egos, a tough guy who engages in macho banter while machine guns fire in the background. It's live radio on the border, and the narcocorridos are popping.

During the 1990s, as the Juárez cartel consolidated its narcotics-trafficking empire and Mexico experienced an unprecedented in-crease in drug violence, the narcocorrido musical genre emerged to chronicle these events and their impact on society. Corridos and drugs have a long history in Mexico. Illegal drugs and the lucrative profits derived from them have been a shady but impor-tant part of the Mexican economy since at least the 1920s. Be-cause the United States is Mexico's major market for narcotics —initially, mainly marijuana and heroin, but more recently also cocaine, methamphetamines, and others—the drug trade has been a major element in the love-hate relationship between the two countries.

Corridos as a musical form can be traced back to the romantic ballad tradition of fourteenth-century Spain. Spanish conquistadores brought this style of music to Mexico, where, by the nineteenth century, it had become a vehicle for expressing and commenting on people's lives, events, and popular sentiments. Especially noteworthy are the corridos about border skirmishes between Mexicans and Anglo Americans and those about the Mexican Revolution; additionally, throughout Mexico, small towns and villages have local corridos. Northern Mexico is best known for corrido production, but it is a type of music made on both sides of the border, wherever Mexican people live, and in other parts of Latin America.

The narcocorrido craze of the 1990s rejuvenated a traditional musical form and gave it the glitz and visibility of *telenovelas* (Mexican soap operas) and rock concerts. The rags-to-riches theme in narcocorridos echoes the central plot of Mexican soap operas, but from a decidedly macho, masculine perspective. The best-known *norteño* groups playing narcocorridos became as popular as Juan Gabriel or the Rolling Stones. Drug trafficking, formerly a profitable and dangerous but primarily underworld phenomenon, had become a pervasive feature of Mexican society and popular culture. Drug lords such as Rafael Caro Quintero and Amado Carillo Fuentes became celebrities just like movie stars. More young Mexicans, not just gringos, began consuming illegal drugs, and the narcostyle of attire (expensive cowboy boots, hats, and belts, flashy silk shirts, and shiny gold jewelry), accoutrements (ostentatious mansions, fancy trucks, and AK-47s), and living tickled the popular imagination.

Despite the profound impact of drugs and narcoculture on Mexican society, narcocorridos are a relatively new and understudied phenomenon in the social sciences. Elijah Wald, a music journalist, hitchhiked all over Mexico to interview the innovative songwriters and singers who created the genre. Wald's brilliant, highly readable account of his journey among the *narcocorridistas* is an essential source of information (Wald 2001; see also Quiñones 2001c for a sophisticated journalistic account of the narcocorrido innovator Chalino Sánchez). José Manuel Valenzuela, in a richly detailed study that focuses on the lyrics and meanings of narcocorridos, provides a major Spanish-language contribution to our understanding of the codes and values that define the narcoworld (Valenzuela 2002). Now, Mark Edberg, using the time-tested methods of anthropological field research, offers a much-needed, grounded perspective on narcocorridos, and the first ethnography in English on this important subject for social analysis. Through fieldwork in neighborhoods, bars, and other social settings in the El Paso/Ciudad Juárez metroplex, Edberg probes the social significance of the hot narcosound. He also researches producers of narcocorridos in a Los Angeles recording company.

Edberg finds that the cultural meanings and impact of narcocorridos are more complex than one might expect from the CD and audiotape covers displaying macho norteños draped in gold chains and wild concert outfits and posing with their trademark accordions and AK-47s. For Edberg the transformation of the classic corrido into the mass media–commodified narcocorrido is not just a celebration of narcotics smuggling, but also a multistranded social process involving the wielding of "thick" symbols that appeal to a diverse Mexican population. That population views the narcotrafficker persona as social bandit heroes in the struggle against poverty, corrupt government, and racist gringos; or as clever entrepreneurs; or as tragic figures in a violent, decadent world; or as entertaining "ghetto-fabulous" *rancheros*; or as symbols of rural Mexican pride in the cities of the United States and Mexico; or simply as the sources and inspiration for clever wordplay, rich sounds, and danceable tunes. Narcocorrido performances and lyrics encode, influence, and enact changing social dynamics in greater Mexico that include shifting gender roles, socioeconomic mobility, international migration, political conflict, ethnic hostilities, and cultural hybridity. Edberg's careful analysis of the polysemic narcocorrido lyrics and narcotrafficker symbols helps us understand this vital aspect of Mexican popular culture and the contemporary music scene along the U.S.-Mexico border.

Acknowledgments

As always, there are more people to acknowledge in the production of a research manuscript than is possible in a brief acknowledgments section. I am "author" of this work only in a limited way—as the person who conceptualized, technically synthesized, and produced the work, even while the ideas, directions, and support came from many sources. Nevertheless, I will attempt to do some justice to these many contributors.

To Drs. George Mentore, Richard Handler, Dell Hymes, and Herbert "Tico" Braun at the University of Virginia, a great many thanks for your support and insights. To the anthropology department at the University of Virginia, I truly appreciate your support throughout. And to June Webb, department secretary, no amount of thanks is enough for all your help.

Without a doubt, none of this would have been possible without the gracious assistance of all those in El Paso and Ciudad Juárez (and thereabouts) who were helpful beyond words: Arturo Herrera Robles and Jessica Peña for taking me everywhere, telling me everything, and helping me with anything, and whose families are like the flowers that will not be prevented from growing even out of the cracks; Dr. Lorenzo and Carmen Lafarelle, for their friendship, for putting me up with fine generosity despite my odd hours, and for contributing many valuable insights, references, and introductions; to their daughter, Margarita, for introducing me to them; to Rafael Núñez, for his wealth of knowledge about El Paso, Juárez, all the strange locations where I might find information, his knowledge and assistance concerning the language, the specialized argots of the border, and the people, and for his general friendship; to Rebecca Ramos and João Ferreira-Pinto (and all at the Compañeros health program) for their friendship and introduction to many who were helpful; to Eddie Hernández and the Back on Track Gang Prevention Program, for his knowledge, his kids, and for making sure

I never wear a thunderbolt earring in Texas; for all their insights and assistance, to Drs. Dennis Bixler-Martínez and Daniel Ortega in the Chicano studies program at the University of Texas at El Paso (UTEP), and Dr. Howard Campbell in the UTEP anthropology department; to Lori and Martin Tapia in Douglas, Arizona, fine *norteño* musicians, for their knowledge of the music and for help in translation; and to Susan Hernández in El Paso, for her knowledge and assistance in setting up interviews.

To the staff at Development Services Group, many thanks for their support, indulgence, and assistance—particularly Alan Bekelman, president; Marcia Cohen, vice president; Katherine Williams, senior associate; and Susan Dunnell, office manager/graphics specialist. And to the Center for Substance Abuse Prevention (Substance Abuse and Mental Health Administration), much appreciation for research support concerning the implications of this work with respect to connections between media images and violence.

Finally, I cannot give enough thanks to my parents and family for their support throughout the entire process, and to my children, Eleazar and Jordana, for teaching me about life and continually asking me, "Dad, when are you going to *finish* this?"

El Narcotraficante

Prologue: Narcocorridos and the Meaning of the Drug Trafficker Image on the U.S.-Mexico Border

Woody Guthrie once asked, "Why do people set down and write great songs and ballads about their outlaws . . . and never about governors, mayors or police chiefs?"[1] The answer is easy. An outlaw is someone "disgusted with trying to live decent in the rich man's system," who tries to "whip the world down to his size" and finds out he cannot, because the world is much bigger than he is. But he tries. He may die trying, but he tries—and "goes down shooting." By contrast, "politicians don't even try. They shoot the bull and the hot air, but they don't try their best to make the world better . . . and the people just don't waste any pencil lead on their politicians, unless it's to write up a song showing how bad they was compared to the outlaw."

There is something compelling about the image of men or women who are willing to risk all against social forces that are stacked against them in the quest for respect. It is an image that resonates in the inventory of enduring cultural representations that make up American culture and Mexican culture in the border region and elsewhere. It is the kind of image long featured in a culturally "thick" narrative and musical genre of northern Mexico and the border region known as the "corrido." Corridos are a discursive form through which heroic values and the situations that frame them have been articulated, particularly since the Mexican-American War in the mid-nineteenth century. However, in the past decade or so, a type of corrido featuring drug traffickers as protagonists has become highly popular in the border region and elsewhere in Mexico, Latin America, and now in parts of the United States. These corridos are often called "narcocorridos," and they are the subject of the research that informed this book.

Since narcocorridos are commonly (though not universally) viewed as within the corrido tradition, an obvious question comes to mind: Are narcotraffickers understood to be of a type with

Pancho Villa, Gregorio Cortez, and the other heroes—both named and unnamed—of past corridos? If so, why? And by whom? The answers to these kinds of questions may say a lot about the nature of this heroic cultural persona, and about the ways in which this persona, and the values and understandings it represents, is mapped onto current circumstances. Moreover, given the military focus of the "drug war," it may also point out a glaring gap in how well Americans understand a situation that is far more complex than is possible to construe under a metaphor of war.

Finally, there is unquestionably a point of view in the literature on narcocorridos (see Chapter 4) that casts them as narratives of resistance, such that the narcotrafficker is discursively framed as a social bandit in the manner described by Hobsbawm (1969), or at least as a trickster or cultural antagonist. My experience conducting this research supports those characterizations to some degree; however, I encountered a much more complex pattern of interpretation, which argues against easy categorization. Moreover, it is clear that the narcotrafficker image as represented in narcocorridos has become *commodified*—because narcocorridos (at least during the period of this research) are popular and a booming business for some record companies and producers. Thus the image is now co-constructed by market forces, a significant contradiction to any interpretation that focuses on narcocorridos solely as populist or resistance narratives.

In any case, it's time to head to the border.

Borderlands: Ciudad Juárez, Chihuahua, and El Paso, Texas

Flying in toward El Paso, as the plane banks around the stark Franklin Mountains, what you see first is a barren crust of earth, which, from the plane, is just barely spotted with scrub brush, as though with a pox. The overwhelming effect is brown. And dry. And brown. And dry. Here and there, ghostly traces of a housing development that was to be—shallow, shadowlike etchings in the dust, laid out in a regular grid of streets and side streets. But no one there. Nothing there. And here and there, the superficial scars of someone's dirt bike treads. All of it is strangely ineffectual, mere timeworn scratches on the leathery skin of a very old face.

I can laugh at myself now, but I thought of El Paso as Old El Paso, a kind of vision, a rich heartland of Mexican American culture. Yes, as a place, El Paso reflects some of that history, to be sure, but in other ways it is a kind of commercial representation long overshadowed by its more workaday role as a place of business on the border. It took some time even to begin to understand. Strangely, I felt that I understood Juárez better, and that I did so right from the beginning. Yet as I became more familiar with El Paso, and many wonderful people who live there, I came to appreciate it on its own terms, not in reference to my vision.

Granted, when I began the research in the summer of 1998, much of Texas was going through a drought and a heat wave, so some of what may have been normal activity was in hiding during the day. Yet my first question, still to some degree unanswered, was, "Where is Old El Paso?" There are a few old-house neighborhoods in the central downtown area, and there is Sunset Heights, a historic district off Mesa Avenue toward UTEP. But the main plaza, the main square—what you would think of as the heart of the city—is small, dusty little San Jacinto Plaza, a block-sized park populated only by a few languid habitués, resting under trees around the famous, but actually very understated, alligator fountain in the center. The rest of the downtown is a somewhat nondescript collection of office buildings, mingled with a few bars and discount clothing stores, except near the Convention Center. There, a small, showpiece urban walk-space around the art museum, Convention Center, and Camino Real hotel has been redone into a modern little enclave clearly tailored to a generic, upscale urban gentry—of which, by the way, there is not much in El Paso. (It is no accident, then, that El Paso's "GQ quarter" is directly adjacent to its poshest hotel.) El Paso is just not a stop on the Starbucks and GQ circuit. Not just yet, anyway. And in any case, the art museum *place d'ambience* dissipates quickly enough. Just down El Paso Street, in the Old El Paso market area, are rows of discount merchandise of all kinds—electronics, T-shirts, clothes, tourist trinkets, handbags. To the west, on Santa Fe Street, is an old border town bus station advertising in painted letters buses heading to Mexicali, Los Angeles, and other destinations. Generally speaking, after work hours, downtown El Paso is just plain empty.

Where, then, is life in El Paso? As I came to learn, El Paso is not a center. It is strung out along Interstate 10, east and west, like grapes clustered to a vine. It is a city of neighborhoods, and it is in those neighborhoods where life takes shape around centers. I first felt this when I happened on a Kermess, a community festival, in a neighborhood somewhere in South El Paso, west of I-10 as it turns south along the border.[2] These festivals are often held at a church or school, and a good percentage of the community comes for some part of the day or evening. At the Kermess, there were booths with games, food, and people selling flea market items and some religious goods. Some of the food was standard festival fare of hot dogs and soft drinks; some was homemade—tamales, taquitos, burritos, and desserts made by the something-auxiliary-club-of-something. And then there was a long lineup of music. When I got there, a band was just finishing up. They played Latino-style rock, the kind of early rock-and-roll that was heavily influenced by 1950s–1960s Chicano culture, like Sam the Sham, or the Mysterians. Next up were four homegirls who had worked out a Spice Girls routine. They had a boombox as backup, turned on taped music sans lyrics, and fronted that little machine with a set of rap-inflected tunes (of their own) in Spanish and a dance act, replete with all the necessary body arching and pouting. I missed the mariachis who had played earlier in the day.

Down on Alameda Avenue in East El Paso, there is also a lot of activity—at night—in the cluster of norteño music bars and clubs in that area. On weekend nights, the parking lots are jammed, especially with trucks of the kind that are popular in the border area, big Suburbans, Dodge Rams, and the like. Inside, the bars and dance floors are crowded with men and women wearing boots, hats, and broad belts. Even with the crowds, though, an outsider walking in may find that more than a few heads turn and tacitly ask the question, "Who are you and what are you doing here?"

Driving along the main line of I-10 at night, El Paso blares at you with its kudzulike overgrowth (or, depending on your point of view, a carnival) of garish signs advertising a sale on this, buy the newest that, motel package stays, discount home furnishings, cars, motorcycles, pizzas, Chinese buffet lunches, the best Mexican food, Toys R Us, on and on. It is a kind of home video American dream, and, indeed, it is set up in part to appeal to consumers coming across the border from Mexico, who are a key customer base, along with all the civilian and military staff and families associated with Fort Bliss and Biggs Army Airfield, a large military base and airfield on El Paso's north side. On Friday nights some of the most popular places to be are the several Wal-Marts—whose parking lots are a great sea of cars, pickup trucks, women trundling babies and bags, and a general chaos of people and things.

Another phenomenon: El Paso has more cheap hotels advertising weekly rates than anywhere I have ever been. What does this mean? Transience, movement, migration. El Paso also has what claims to be the world's largest Harley-Davidson dealership. Again, movement and migration. It is, after all, the borderland. At the same time, underneath the transient overlay, there are a lot of people

Plate 1. The Rio Grande between El Paso, Texas, and Ciudad Juárez, Chihuahua.

who have lived in El Paso for a long time, and whose families and extended relationships span both sides of the border. It is the social core.

Just across the bridge over the anticlimactic Rio Grande—manhandled in its drab, gray cement channel—Ciudad Juárez is something quite different (Plate 1). Juárez is chaotic, even vaguely menacing at first. Dusty. Dirty. Taxis, belching cars, painted buses, Tarahumara Indian women and little children selling tourist trinkets of various descriptions, and people walking everywhere, with babies, with packages, on sidewalks that are obstacle courses (of holes, some boarded-up, some not, exposed pipes never quite repaired, etc.), in the plaza with its old Spanish church (Plates 2a and b). But at least there are people. Walking, talking, laughing, standing, waiting for buses. For all its harshness, there is an energy in Juárez that is palpable.

And the river. The infamous, or fabled, Rio Grande. Yet here, it is eviscerated, rendered soulless between its dusty, gray cement banks, barely distinguishable in tonality from the relentless and thrumming functionality of the interstate just to the north. Atop the riverbank on both sides, a chain-link fence, crowned in barbed

Plates 2a and b. Central plaza in the old section of Juárez and typical Juárez bus.

wire, fronting a dirt road that parallels the river and appears mainly to be used by Border Patrol or Mexican police. One day, I saw three men wading across in the muddy water, holding clothes (or something else indeterminable from the viewpoint of the bridge) above their heads, in full view of everyone, including, presumably, the Mexican police. They were wading underneath the train trestle, with its huge iron gate midway across designed to thwart use by migrants. On the U.S. side, two green Border Patrol ("Migra") trucks sat on the dirt road, right next to the trestle. Did the men not see the trucks? At some point they must have, because they scuttled up the bank and hid underneath the bridge.

And the chaos. A large pothole in the road, repaired with a junked car door and a tree limb. On a long street lined with buildings and shops close to crumbling or being blown off into the desert, a brand-new high-rise hotel in fresh pastel colors. Why there? And Avenida Juárez—where at every corner you are approached with overdramatic, yet hushed, questions: "Boystown? Want to go to Boystown? What kinda women you like? You want some pills? What do you like?"—only a block away from a street lined with bridal shops, beauty academies, dentists' offices, and pharmacies. Contrast this with the glitzy PRONAF (Programa Nacional Fronterizo, National Border Program) area around Avenida 16 Septiembre and López Mateos, with its glass-faced buildings, restaurants, banks, and, not far away, American-style malls.

And the poverty. In the concentric sprawl of colonias near parts of the city center and in an ever-widening circle around it, the outer boundary of which seems to fizzle out into the bone-dry desert, at which point the mud-colored colonia dwellings and the desert appear almost as one and the same. Amid the ostensible economic boon from the *maquilas,*[3] the colonias are the other side of the equation, pouring forth workers on early-morning buses and taking them back in the evening, to the dirt-road, scrap, and cement neighborhoods, some of which have been part of Juárez for a long time, others of which are more recent additions to accommodate the substantial numbers of migrants heading up to the borderlands. Many of these colonias go by mellifluous names that border on the surreal —Colonia Bella Vista (Beautiful View), Colonia Revolución (Revolution), Colonia Alta Vista (High View).

El Paso, Juárez. Juárez, El Paso. So different, yet tendrils of one so rooted in the other—families with cousins on one side, brothers just across the Rio Grande. Back and forth; here for one thing, there for another.

It was in this setting that I began trundling myself and a small backpack with notebooks, a tape recorder, and bottled water back and forth across the Santa Fe bridge—in step, I suppose, in some small way with all the others. In those treks back and forth across the bridge, back and forth from Juárez to El Paso (and later to other parts of the border area in Arizona and California), I recorded some distinct impressions about the place, the setting, as a way of trying to become aware, in the limited way that I could, of the kinds of sights, sounds, and cues that form part of the background for how daily events are interpreted. This was a way of introducing myself to a complex setting within which I sought to investigate the cultural image of the narcotrafficker as it is played out in narcocorridos.

Generally, the notion of a border zone as a growing ground for narcocorridos may best be viewed under a broader definition, less tied to the actual geographic border—especially since narcocorridos are known and written well beyond the border (and in Mexico, certain states in the sierra or near the Pacific coast, such as Sinaloa, are well-known narcotrafficker territory and thus the origin of many a narcocorrido). Still, however it is imagined, it could be said that the border is a distiller of themes and a metaphoric region of ambiguity—a liminal space. It is a zone of conflict, a zone of movement and transition, a zone of both harsh poverty and fantastic wealth, a zone where there is a "thin line between love and hate," but also a zone where normal life exists, on its own terms. Among many impressions recorded in my field notes are the following:

The first time I crossed the Santa Fe bridge into Juárez, over the broad cement channel that is the fabled Rio Grande (or Río Bravo) at that point, I looked down and saw graffiti on the sloping, dusty, gray channel wall—far more prosaic than one would imagine for the banks of the Rio Grande. On one wall some of the graffiti read as follows:

¡¡¡Ya basta!!!
Por cada ilegal que nos maltraten
En los Estados Unidos de N.A.
Vamos a maltratar
Un visitante gabacho
"Bienvenidos los paisanos"

This translates, more or less, as "Enough! For every illegal mistreated in the United States, we will mistreat one gringo visitor. Welcome, countrymen!"

¡¡Ojo migra!!
533-4346
Para reportar abusos

This translates as "Watch out, INS [or Border Patrol]! 533-4346, to report abuses."

9 de mayo del 91
Tarin, descansa en paz
Querido amigo siempre
Te recordaremos
Tus compas del PN
y de tu madre

This piece of graffiti is a little less clear, but translates as "May 9, 1991. Tarin, rest in peace. Dear friend always. We will remember you—your PN [Partido Nacional] friends and from your mother." Does it refer to someone who died crossing the river?

Another day, as I crossed the bridge, I looked back toward the graffiti and it was set against a row of green Border Patrol trucks parked on the dirt road that immediately parallels the river, above the banks and behind a chain-link fence crowned with barbed wire. The overall image was quite stark, though I must consider my own reaction as a visitor to the situation, in contrast to that of residents who see this kind of picture all the time and for whom it may be mere background noise. And yet, as I surveyed the setting, a constant stream of people flowed back and forth across the bridge, many of those returning to the Mexican side trundling along with bags of purchased goods. It is, as best I can tell, a kind of love-hate relationship.

Then there are the sprawling colonias both near the central part of the city and on the outskirts. These colonias have euphemistic names such as "Bella Vista," or "Alta Vista," or "Revolución," that belie their crumbling, dusty poverty. One day, I went out to Colonia Revolución with Jorge (pseudonym), a member of Cuauhtémoc Cárdenas' Partido de la Revolución Democrática and health outreach worker for a Juárez-based drug and HIV/AIDS program. I was going to interview two youth, but before that I spent time in a community meeting where colonia residents of a particular "block" were discussing a petition they were going to sign and present requesting that the municipal government pave their dirt streets. The houses along the street were all small, cubelike, and makeshift in character, some constructed of what looked like scrap wood and other scrap materials, others appearing somewhat more permanent, built using cinderblocks along with a patchwork of miscellaneous items for roofing and fences. The streets were dirt, occasionally embedded with old discarded tires and metal scraps. A scruffy, anemic dog ambled up the street. At one house around the corner, a lime-green golf cart was parked in a loosely built wood enclosure—car and garage. All those I talked to at the meeting said that they worked at various maquilas. Their typical pay rate was the equivalent of about $30–$40 per week; at that time, though, it must be noted that the peso was in a continual slide, so even that equivalent amount would be less within a matter of weeks.

At the same time, in one colonia I noticed a house that stood out as unusual at the end of a long row of dwellings in the manner I described above. It was a permanent, constructed house, with a fence, windows, a front yard—much like a small American suburban home. Why was this house here? I was told that the owner was probably involved in the drug trade at some point, and that he most likely used the money he made to set up or buy the small car repair shop and eatery on the corner near his house. He may or may not still be involved in the trade, but, either way, the drug money had served as "development money" or investment capital of a sort. It is not an uncommon story.

In contrast to the poverty of the colonias, I also took a tour of the "other side" in Juárez. There was, for example, a family "compound" of one of the elite ruling families in Juárez. The compound was a strange sight, a virtual walled city with ornate walls so high it was not possible to see anything but the tops of palm trees inside. Yet the compound sits in an ugly industrial park area. There is no neighborhood around at all. The closest sign of activity other than traffic and a small mini-mall with shops and a restaurant is a dirt lot, devoid of any vegetation and strewn here and there with glinting glass shards, on which a few children were playing soccer.

Nearby, there is a residential area known as El Campestre, in which the houses are often garish in their façades, very much like some houses in Beverly Hills, with ornate Greek columns and multicolored domes, or palatial in the manner of a

European estate. Some had imposing walls and gates, and I saw one that was clearly equipped for a high level of security, with several manned guard stations. Right next to this neighborhood is a section called "Rincones de San Marcos," which has been dubbed "Rincones de San Narcos" because of all the narco-traffickers who are said to live there. Narcotrafficker families and other wealthy families in these neighborhoods, I understand, mix without much problem, despite what may be differences in class origin. Maybe money is just money.

A short distance away, and close to one of the only remaining ejidos[4] in Juárez, is a walled and gated community called Misión de los Lagos. The former governor of the State of Chihuahua keeps a house there . . .

1. Corridos, Cultural Representations, and Poverty

Before reviewing research results concerning the interpretation of narcocorridos and the construction of the narcotrafficker persona, let us consider some basic questions and issues. Assessing narcocorridos and their representations of the narcotrafficker is a useful study in the process of cultural-image construction, dissemination, and transformation. In addition, however, such an assessment may inform broader questions concerning the interaction between poverty, viewed within a context of social stratification, and cultural processes. What does a shared, ongoing condition of poverty and subordinate status do with respect to the systems of signification, symbolic fields, identity, and notions of self, discourse, and day-to-day practice that we call "culture"?

This is, of course, not a novel question. Issues of poverty and social marginality have long been a concern of anthropology. In an urban or village context, this lineage includes at least the various "Chicago school" ethnographies (e.g., N. Anderson 1923; Thrasher 1927; Spradley 1970, 1972), the "slum" studies of William Foote Whyte (1993), studies on ethnicity and stratification in American cities (e.g., Warner and Srole 1945; Warner and Lunt 1947; Warner 1959), the "culture of poverty" series (Lewis 1966, 1975; Lewis and Butterworth 1968), Liebow's street corner society (1967), George Foster's studies of Mexican village life in Tzintzuntzán (1967), Leeds' holistic studies of urban social structure (see Sanjek 1994), Labov's studies of class, language, and "Black English Vernacular" (1966, 1972), Stack's urban reciprocity networks (1974), studies of squatter settlements (e.g., Epstein 1972), Agar's research with urban heroin addicts (1973), Hannerz' work on urban culture and creolization (1980, 1987, 1989), Ogbu's investigation of minority cultural models and school performance (1990), Bourgois' look at respect and the crack trade (1989, 1996), and Fleisher's work with youth gangs (1998). Much of this work has involved rich descriptive ethnography of cultural patterns in their relation to social conditions, descriptions of attitudes, values, and beliefs, and more macro-level descriptions of social structures and patterns of spatial organization associated with urban poverty (Gmelch and Zenner 1996). In addition, work focusing on the subaltern (e.g., Spivak 1988) within the body of postcolonial studies has been an important influence on this topic area. Indeed, Marcus (1998, p. 85) notes that all ethnography concerned with the world system "habitually focuses upon subaltern subjects, those positioned by systemic domination (ultimately traceable to capitalist and colonialist political economy in its variety of forms)."

It is well known that the body of work focusing on relationships between culture and poverty in the 1950s and 1960s was roundly criticized for, among other transgressions, formulating a homogeneous "trait list" which was posited as defining a distinct and objectified "culture of poverty" said to be passed down generationally among families that were among the long-term poor, for not adequately examining the dynamics of interaction between people and structural conditions (lack of employment, racism, etc.), and for ignoring data that did not fit the model (see Goode and Eames 1996). Other research on poverty and modernization during the same period (e.g., McClelland 1961; Inkeles and Smith 1964) has also been criticized heavily for imposing static and ethnocentric criteria used in evaluating the "progress" and "modernization" of non-Western societies.

The present research, however, is not a revision, repeat, or rehash of these efforts. Instead, it is an attempt to focus on identity and representation—on the ways in which poverty and social stratification intertwine with the formation and dissemination of cultural representations, including the ways in which such representations are disseminated and take meaning from the mass media. To do this, the research summarized herein falls in significant ways under the kind of ethnographic approach categorized by Marcus (1998, p. 83) as "multi-sited ethnography," because it is "the cultural formation," potentially produced in several different locales, "rather than the conditions of a particular set of subjects that is the object of study." Moreover, "the idea is that any cultural identity or activity is constructed by multiple agents in varying contexts, or places . . . and ethnography must be strategically conceived to represent this multiplicity" (p. 52). As noted by Ulf Hannerz (1987, as quoted by Marcus 1998, p. 51; emphasis added), the world has become more like one network of social relationships, "*and between its different regions there is a flow of meanings as well as of people and goods.*"

Moreover, as John Thompson has argued (1995, p. 75)—extending notions of the "public sphere" described by Habermas—the large-scale commercialization of mass media has altered the character of this public sphere, both in the way that media representations are dominated by their position as commodities, and because "individuals are able to interact with others and observe persons and events without ever encountering them in the same spatial-temporal locale." The latter supports Marcus' contention that there is a need for an ethnography that accounts for a disconnect between representations and interpersonal interaction.

In an applied sense, this research was motivated in part by my experience in health and social intervention and prevention projects with inner-city urban populations that have largely been in subordinate—or subaltern, if you will—socioeconomic positions. Practices that are classified using a trope of risk (as "risk behavior") by these public health or other intervening agencies are often enacted by those involved from their very different social positions and thus (often) with different interpretive tools. While working on these projects, it has been abundantly clear to me (from project clients' narratives and conversations, as well as their daily life patterns) that these interpretive tools include shared, commonsense understandings concerning subordinate, alienated, or marginalized social position, and what that position entails with respect to identity, constructions of self—and the cultural representations that are part of such constructions—and day-to-day as well as long-term decisions about how to lead a life. In short, the risk behavior is situated in, and draws meaning from, representations concerning the context of stratification. A better understanding of these representations and interpretive tools may result in better approaches for addressing urban health and social issues.

There are considerable difficulties in finding commonalities of definition and meaning surrounding this issue. The concepts of subordinate/subaltern social status, and the term "poverty," are terminally elusive and amorphous. The meaning of these concepts is relative. Are we talking about material conditions? Class? Potential "mobility" between classes? A state of being that exists within a discourse of social valuation constructed from a specific configuration of power? A node within a political ecology of hegemony, exploitation, and domination? Or simply one pole of a structural pair in a semantic field that in turn rolls through a social field like a magic stone, configuring everything as an endless series of homologies around some concept of social differentiation? In a sense, it is all of these things and more. It is *not* just occupation, *not* just income, wealth, ownership of capital, or any other material factor. It is also a symbolic category. The juxtaposition of the indeterminancy and the tangibility of the issue is one major reason why the several interested academic disciplines have had a hard time pinning it down. It is also one reason that questions of poverty and social inequality have been such cannon fodder for political and ideological agendas.

All the clutter notwithstanding, small stories still have a way of encapsulating the heart of the matter. I have in mind a number of these that have remained with me since I worked on a series of street-based projects concerning HIV/AIDS (largely, now, a disease of poverty), violence, drug abuse, dropping out of school, and other such issues. For example,

> STORY ONE: Two older addicts are talking on the corner, one sitting on a chair, the other standing. I am listening to what I can pick up of their conversation. They are talking about "the life," that is, the way of life that centers on use of (and addiction to) heroin, cocaine, and whatever else, and the whole process of getting and selling the drugs and negotiating all the interactions and relationships involved. More than that, they seem to be talking about what it all *means.* The conversation consists of reminiscing, and one baiting the other about what they used to do, or one boasting to the other about what they used to do, in approximately the following form:
> A: Hey, I used ta' take [amount of drug] and still be able to [perform some action].
> B: Naaaw. I never saw that!
> A: Doncha remember when we [did some action x when we had taken some amount of drug Y]??

Why was this conversation, this story, interesting? Because the central issue seemed to be one of *mastery,* about a time when their drug use was the vehicle and the metaphor by which to show how they could "get over," how they could "fend off a challenge" from the drug (as if it were a rival, a challenger, a competitor) without losing a step as a man, as a master of the universe. Like warfare, the courtroom, the boardroom, the bedroom, or the family room, "the life" was just one more in the human continuum of arenas on which to play out one's story, one's triumphs and defeats, one's place in the cosmos. It was, it seemed, the arena that for these men was the most accessible in their lives. One could also describe this as a narrative field, a piece of "carved out" discursive territory in which personal power can be enacted, even while that narrative field is nested within an overall structure of disempowerment.[1]

I was also told that if someone overdoses on a street corner, other junkies will rush to the corner to see if they can get hold of whatever the overdoser was using. It's kind of a challenge: to try and play against the odds with something that will take you so far. And when they talk about the one who overdosed, they might even say that he was just *incompetent*—he couldn't take it. He wasn't a master of the game.

> STORY TWO: In a shelter for youth in trouble, I was talking to a fifteen-year-old African American boy as part of a study on HIV risk and substance abuse. Like many of the other youth I spoke with who came from Southeast and other economically depressed sections of Washington, D.C., he was heavily involved in the ubiquitous street economy, which, of course, includes the drug market, but many other activities as well. In some places, this is the economy that counts. This is what is real. After reciting his various "jobs"—stealing cars, acting as a drug-dealer's lookout, and so on—he smiled and said, "See, I know how to make money without carrying people's bags."

I took that to be a statement about at least one of the meanings the "work" he described had for him. It was a matter of pride to him that he knew how to obtain resources without being in a constant position of subordination to do so. He was, in his piece of the world, on top for a change.

> STORY THREE: In a tiny house in poverty-ridden Colonia Revolución in Ciudad Juárez, Mexico, I sat on a couch and talked to an eighteen-year-old boy (approximate age) who lolled his head from time to time, drowsy from the heroin he used regularly. When we started talking about narcotraffickers— about whether or not they were viewed as heroes—he immediately perked up and, as we spoke, seemed to transform from a semisomnolent addict into a young man who owned the world. He didn't have to say much about what the image of the narcotrafficker meant to him. It was obvious. He swayed from side to side, snapped his fingers, and his mouth opened into a sly smile. For him, this image was power, efficacy, the ability to have things and do things that were far out of reach in a life

that stood in clear contrast to that fantasy. There was little doubt that he would be one if he could.

In these kinds of narratives, people are structuring the way in which various practices—practices often linked strongly with serious poverty—have meaning for them. And, it is through this narrative field that an opportunity exists to improve understanding of this world, this "habitus" or "figured world" (see Holland et al. 1998), if you will, so that others can participate in the tasks of change. In the description of the research on narcocorridos that follows, I attempt to look at one very small piece of this narrative field, connected to a particular sociocultural setting, with the express intent of examining, as best I can, the linkages between the narratives and what they represent within a context of poverty and social stratification, nested within a macrocontext of modern mass media.

Social Stratification and Subjectivity

First, it is important to set out what I mean with respect to social stratification, because it is not cultural representations associated with poverty per se that I am interested in, but those associated with situations of poverty understood by most participants (in the situation) to exist within a socially stratified context. This statement may seem without point, given that a condition of poverty can almost always be shown to exist (following Wallerstein and many others) as part of an overall structure or structures of domination and subordination. Let me clarify it this way: When I refer to poverty per se, I am referring to the bare, objective fact of living with limited resources, scarce food supplies, and so on, *which may or may not be construed by participants as "poverty."* The distinction is that of the subject, and thus underlies how people represent their situation, however insufficient that may be as a comprehensive explanation or description. Moreover, I am going to use "social stratification" as a reference term, knowing its inadequacies, specifically because I do not want to subsume this research entirely within the postcolonial-studies narrative of the subaltern. That would lock it into presupposed interactional relationships of domination-accommodation or domination-resistance in a way that I would rather not do at the outset.

First, however, let us look briefly at a range of theoretical constructs commonly used to treat the existence of a pattern of stratification. As a first caveat, I acknowledge that most concepts and terminologies used across various disciplines to discuss this issue are, on their face, bound up in the trope of holism, of static wholes, so amply deconstructed by Marcus and Fischer (1986; Marcus 1998). Nevertheless, a review is necessary to establish a reference point for discussion. As a base, such constructs are typically concerned with some organized system of social inequality, whether that inequality is viewed from a positive, a negative, or simply a neutral or functional standpoint (see Grusky 1994). The inequality is most often described as manifested through a particular positional matrix, in which "higher social positions" are associated with both a greater number of rewards (e.g., status, resources, prestige) and power—as these are culturally defined—than are "lower positions." Some theoretical approaches go beyond merely a positional framework, because a positional approach is clearly inadequate to describe the full nature of stratification. In addition, various theoretical constructs focus on specific kinds of power and reward connected to the range of positions across or within societies, what the cultural criteria are for particular positional matrices, the fluidity of particular positional matrices ("social mobility"), and the ways in which a particular system is reproduced and represented over time.

Stratification as Hierarchy

While the terms "stratification" and "hierarchy" are often conflated, they may also have different implications, flowing from two contrasting constructions of the relationship between individuals and society. Dumont (1980, 1986) draws the distinction between *societas* and *universitas.* The former term refers to the Western paradigm in which the individual exists prior to society (e.g., as expounded by Rousseau and Hobbes), where society is a change from the natural state and a voluntary organization *composed of individuals.* "Universitas" refers to the understanding that society exists prior to individuals, that individuals are constituted, as human beings, from society. In the latter, holistic view, a hierarchical system such as the caste system in India is not valorized based on the situations of individuals (or groups of individuals), but only in terms of the organizing principles of the whole—in the case of India, relationships of purity/impurity replicated throughout the system, according to Dumont. Thus hierarchy cannot be viewed as a linear progression according to some value or criterion (as in the European Christian conception of the "Great Chain of Being") but as the *encompassing* of a value and its contrary within all relationships in a system. Assuming that this has at least some validity for India (an argument that has its critics), this means that the social and material situations of individuals are simply an inevitable and necessary expression of the whole.

Stratification as Rank

The term "rank" has generally been used in anthropology to describe societies that, during a particular historical period, increased their productive capacity through more intensive agricultural or other production techniques and technologies, grew in size, and, in so doing, developed more-or-less fixed systems of graded ranks—high chief, chief, warrior, and the like—that are typically ascribed, or kinship based. Such ranked systems typically involve a differential in wealth and goods by rank, but this is often balanced to some degree by the obligation of higher ranks to redistribute wealth or provide some form of public service. Ranks are not necessarily associated with ownership of productive resources (see, e.g., Berreman and Zaretsky 1981; Helms 1979). The notion of rank is not significantly relevant to the concept of stratification at issue in this book.

Stratification as Class

Stratification is much more typically used in connection with class analysis. The differences here are related to the way in which class is defined. The two archetype conceptual poles in this regard flow from Marx and Weber. In the traditional Marxist sense, "class," of course, refers to a social group that exists by virtue of its relationship to the means of production, and whose motivation and identity (class consciousness) is based on shared material interests. This concept is already inadequate in terms of handling the complexity of economic and occupational situations in modern industrial capitalism, and even more inadequate in addressing issues of race or ethnicity or cultural meaning, which cut across strict economic categories (see also West 1993, p. 267), yet may play a role in determining stratification.

On a macroscale (see, e.g., Wallerstein 1979), this approach has evolved into theory of and discussions about the world system of global capitalism—generally structured as a center and periphery in the system as a whole, and within nations as well. The center refers to the socioeconomic complex of industrialized countries or transnational corporations that control productive forces and the global financial system, and thus create an exploitative relationship with so-called Third World or producer countries that, in large measure, supply the raw materials—and now labor—to the system of production.

"Class" in the Weberian sense refers almost to an "inflection" on individuals—differences in "life chances" determined by such "causal components" as property, skills, and education as these influence mobility in the market system (Grusky 1994; Weber 1994; Crompton 1993). Where there is a grouping of individuals who share similar "life chances" and within which individual and generational mobility is shared and typical, this is a "class." This formulation does not carry the same sense of group consciousness as does class in the Marxist sense. However, note that Weber does differentiate between class and status groups, and the latter type of grouping, discussed below, is based on more subjective notions of position.

Stratification and Subjectivity

Of much more use for purposes of the present research are concepts of stratification that focus more on the subjective, culturally constructed ways in which a pattern of stratification is understood and represented by individuals or groups within and between particular social strata.[2] With respect to class concepts in this general category, I noted above that Weber (1994) describes status as a principle of positional group formation that is sometimes coterminous, but sometimes competing, with class as typically defined. Status groups are rooted in their shared type of "social esteem," or *honor*, bestowed upon them, as expressed in a particular lifestyle. The latter, in the sense of Bourdieu, can simply be seen as a symbolic enactment of the semiotics of social position.

Class itself is defined more broadly and subjectively by Bourdieu, E. P. Thompson, and Gramsci. For Bourdieu (1977, 1986, 1987) there are four different forms of capital—economic, cultural, social, and symbolic—"which together empower (or otherwise) agents in their struggle for position within 'social space'" (Crompton 1993, p. 173). "As a consequence of these different empowerments, individual classes come to develop and occupy a similar habitus, 'understood as a system of dispositions shared by all individuals who are products of the same conditionings'" (Crompton 1993, p. 173; Bourdieu 1987, p. 762). E. P. Thompson (1968, p. 10) argues that class is not a category or structural unit, but a consciousness related to productive relations—the way these relations are "handled in cultural terms: embodied in traditions, value—systems, ideas, and institutional forms." Finally, for Gramsci (1971), class is related to culture and ideology, in the degree to which groups actively consent or do

not consent to the ideology of the dominant class.[3] Class is therefore a *process* of struggle between "cultural modalities" (Hall 1981,
cited in Crompton 1993) on a local and global level.

Extending this position is Foucault, whose general discussion of
power (see, e.g., 1972, 1973, 1975, 1979, 1980a, 1980b) centers on the
way in which dominant discursive practices, at a given point in history, incorporate and implement definitions of truth, validity, nor-
mality, deviance, social esteem, and other elements of a specific
episteme. The dominant discourse flows from the historically contingent role of particular institutions in society—which does not,
however, necessarily come about as a result of conscious efforts at
dominance (in contrast to a strict or "canned" Marxist formulation).
At a given time, then, the level of dominance by any one or several
social units entails a dialectical process in which the dominant discourse "reigns," so to speak, but is also contested from "points of resistance" within that society. Without overly stretching the matter,
we can say that the dominant discourse concerning social position
in the United States and most Western industrialized societies follows the ex post facto logic of Calvinist capitalism (see Weber 1958)
in which the social valorization of individuals is tied to their level
of material accumulation, as well as the degree to which they have
control over various components of capital (including social, symbolic, and cultural capital). Further, these characteristics are natu-
ralized as *moral,* as manifestations of the internal qualities of individuals or groups.

The key position of the commercial media industry as a purveyor
and shaper of public images and transcultural social groupings (e.g.,
"world youth") may be just one of these institutional formations
that creates a dominant discourse in which public images are both
cultural representations and commodities. This, as I will discuss
later, will play a central role in what narcocorridos are as a current
iteration of the corrido genre.

With this in mind, discourses of identity as related to social
stratification occur at several levels and at both formal and informal occasions. They contain references, assumptions, characterizations, and explanations concerning the ontologies of defined sociocultural groups that are highly represented in particular places in
the stratified system—by extension, referring to individuals who
primarily identify themselves as members of a given group x. Such
discourses may also encode an explanatory paradigm about how the
world works, why things are, what one can expect a life to consist
of (as a member of a group x and an individual in the larger society),
norms or codes of comportment, and so on. With respect to strati-

fication, these discourses contain *meanings* and criteria associated with place in the system, and as such have an inherent *evaluative* and *referential* power. They are cultural material that shape what Holland et al. (1998) call "figured worlds."

The discourse takes shape in everyday conversations about why something happened or what someone is going to do regarding some circumstance. Or, it exists in songs, stories, and humor, such as in the narcocorridos that are the subject of this research, and the meanings given to symbolic objects of daily life. It also appears as more formalized mythic text about the origins of group x and legendary figures (or lack of) in group x's history, and in ritual text. As Maschio (1994) has noted, mythic text objectifies experience within a shared context and provides the stuff from which individual identities draw. These are the "grand stories" or scripts, or "paradigm scenarios" (de Sousa 1990) that affect how individuals feel about who they are in the world, a domain integrally connected to stratification.

The process linking stratified position and cultural identity has also been addressed by Riesman (1992) from a symbolic interactionist perspective (see Mead 1964). Relevant to this discussion is Riesman's description of a dialectic of Self versus Other that is informed by everyday and formal discourse that frames the *difference* (between Self and Other) in terms of stratification. That such discourse can have a significant effect on shared identity and the shape of cultural practices has been shown, for example, in Riesman's analysis of differences between Fulani and RiimaayBe self-characterizations in West Africa (Riesman 1992).

Discourses of stratification (or the subjectivity thereof) are also inherent in the general postcolonial dialogue concerning the subaltern (see, e.g., Said), in which the focus is on the experience, the subjectivity of the subaltern under a colonial or postcolonial framework, where that subjectivity is cast as resistance to dominant structures and discourse, and where the project is in part an attempt to reveal the one-sided, self-interested, and discursively constructed portrayal (in Western texts) of peoples and social situations in the non-European world.

Identity and Representation: Theoretical Underpinnings

I do not want to linger on definitions of stratification, because, as noted, I employ these here primarily as a foundation for a focus on identity and representation. To "get at" issues of identity and representation with respect to the goals of this study, I draw from several theoretical influences. First, the definitional focus of culture as *representation*—an emphasis on culture as exerting influence via a "system of signification" or representation (see, e.g., Geertz 1983; Sperber 1996)—in which shared understandings about the nature of the world, the basic underpinnings of action, reside over time in shared, socially distributed aggregations[4] or inventories of representations (at a given time) that develop historically within and across specific societies and groups.

Second is Marcus' (1998) critique (building on Marcus and Fischer 1986) of the traditional ethnographic trope of culture as tied to a "place." A broader, or multisited, research imaginary allows fieldwork to follow the "complex spaces" that are more reflective of the wider systemic influences on cultural practices and representations, and the wider field in which those practices and representations are actually distributed (see also Rosaldo 1989 on intracultural variation and fluidity). Related to this are the range of discussions on nationalist and transnational identity (e.g., B. Anderson 1983; Hobsbawm 1990; Gilroy 1993; also Fanon 1968) that describe other processes and levels of discourse involved in the construction of identity beyond and between categories of nation, place, dominant/ subordinate oppositions, and beyond facile definitions of race and ethnicity (Hall [1989] 1995). Thus the "available representations" of self include those derived from the immediate social context, those that are transcultural (transnational) in the current global context (Hannerz 1989), and those derived from ethnic/nationalist discourse. This is not to say that transcultural representations of self do not intersect with dominant/subordinate factors either locally or on a global scale (Hannerz 1987).

Third is the proposition that the concept of a "self" is a socially constructed, intersubjective, symbolic phenomenon incorporating culturally and transculturally shared understandings about boundaries of existence and intention as they relate to individual persons, about relationships between individual and group, between individuals as group members and those defined as others, and standards or processes by which individuals become full persons, gendered persons, and so on (see Marsella, DeVos, and Hsu 1985; Carrithers, Collins, and Lukes 1985; Leenhardt 1979). Individuals form a notion of self from the available cultural representations and rhetorics of "selfness"; becoming a self involves a dialog between individual, particular experience and collective representations for experience (Battaglia 1995; Bakhtin 1981; Holland et al. 1998), as well as the *performance* of the "represented self" in day-to-day life (see also Goffman 1959).

Fourth is Bourdieu's (1977) connection between representation and action—the framing of life situation as an ongoing dialectic between the social structure as historically developed and its dominant discourse, on the one hand, and daily practice, on the other. This forms what Bourdieu calls a *"habitus."* For Bourdieu, individuals who are in a similar position within a social structure[5] share "convergent experiences" in terms of the actual, day-to-day economic and social constraints that position imposes on how one can live a life. These constraints intertwine with the process of representing self (identity) to form a kind of reflexive cycle in which the constrained pattern of daily life is reinforced by, and understood in terms of, representations about who one is in relation to the social structure. In terms of the proposed research, this suggests that what individuals in a subordinate social position do and *can do* in daily life (given the social, economic, and other constraints of their position within the stratified system)—that is, the selves they make— will be understood via available representations, including the predominance of those from the dominant discourse. What they *do* will thus be framed in representations about *who they are.* Bourdieu notes that this process of representation exists as "commonsense" understanding, or a "logic of practice," as opposed to an abstracted or conscious process. The process is also embodied—as a "bodily hexis," or social mnemonic—in the seemingly insignificant details of an individual's physical presentation (Bourdieu 1977).

In summary, I approach the research with the understanding that an important dimension of stratification involves a symbolic discourse of social categorization under which status is constructed and contested around the ways in which individual attributes (e.g., culture, racial/ethnic features, income/wealth, speech styles, purported work habits, lifestyle patterns, values, and family structure) are represented.

Yet these representations are also inhabited by individuals in everyday life, and thus the second key dimension is *performance.* The pattern of stratification is manifested, and evolves, through the ways in which it is practiced and embodied by individuals on a daily basis, and the ways in which that daily practice (Bourdieu's habitus) is coded, shaped by, and reinforces or contests the dominant discourse (as it relates to stratification). As noted earlier, while the research discussed herein was undertaken primarily on the U.S.-Mexico border, the processes involved may be similar in many situations outside the context of this particular research effort (see Riesman 1992; DeVos and Suárez-Orozco 1990).

2. Investigating Narcocorridos and Their Meaning in the U.S.-Mexico Border Context

As a particular case in which some of the general concerns mentioned in Chapter 1 may be elucidated, the research on narcocorridos is intended as a preliminary investigation regarding their role, in combination with social conditions, in shaping the creation of a cultural archetype or persona—the narcotrafficker—and the pattern of action that ties violence, power, money, and drugs to political, social, and regional themes for which the narcotrafficker is known.[1] Produced and distributed through well-known yet "underground" channels, these songs feature archetypal heroes, or "big men," who are involved in the drug trade, smuggling, drug use, or other related activity that is prevalent on the border. Building on the corrido tradition—border ballads with epic themes of heroes who resisted the Texas Rangers, U.S. authorities, or, in some cases, even central Mexican authorities (Paredes 1958, 1993; Herrera-Sobek 1993)—these new corridos have situated their protagonists in the current border context and have gained substantial popularity among a wide range of Mexican, Mexican American, and other Hispanic audiences. For some narcocorrido groups (e.g., Los Tucanes de Tijuana or Los Tigres del Norte),[2] the audience has broadened beyond Mexico to Latin America at large.

Like some "gangsta rap" or early reggae, the narcocorridos often describe the exploits of, and situations faced by, those who are portrayed in some manner as outlaw heroes, or "social bandits" (Hobsbawm 1969). A basic presumption, therefore, is the following: the fact that these songs are in corrido form has significance with respect to their meaning and the meaning of the narcotrafficker character they so often feature.

For purposes of this research, I was generally interested in the following:

- How are these narcocorridos framed or understood by those who listen to them and those who produce them? Both groups have been included in this study under the assumption that the meanings commonly drawn from a given media product result from a synthesis of producer and consumer motives, goals, and interpretive frameworks.

- How do the narcocorridos shape or reflect common understandings of the narcotrafficker—particularly in terms of the way the narcotrafficker is situated in the context of broader social forces in the U.S.-Mexico border area, which include patterns of social stratification?
- Do narcocorridos, as a vehicle for representing the narcotrafficker, have any impact on patterns of individual action, including violence and involvement in trafficking? And, finally,
- Are the answers to these questions generalizable to broader questions regarding the influence of public (including media) representations on individual action?

Of course, in a small-scale, preliminary study such as this, I do not expect definitive answers. What I hope for is more at the level of the suggestive, which can at least provide directions for further research.

Research Site and Rationale

I conducted the research primarily in two sites, following the general division between producers and consumers of the narcocorridos. The bulk of interviews and observations were conducted in the twin cities of El Paso, Texas, and Ciudad Juárez, Chihuahua, which straddle the border in West Texas. Together, El Paso and Juárez form an urban area with a population of more than two million. The El Paso/Juárez metropolitan area is a major urban border center, characterized by significant poverty (e.g., in the colonias, slums or shack settlements) and visible wealth, due to the dominant presence of maquila (cross-border) industries and the drug trade. It also has a relatively high rate of drug use, including injection use.

I also conducted a small number of interviews in Los Angeles, California, because that metropolitan area is the site of offices and studios for a number of the major producers, distributors, and marketers of narcocorridos and related music—including EMI Records (EMI-Latin) and Fonovisa and several smaller companies, such as Cintas Acuario Internacional. In addition, the Los Angeles area could be characterized as a "hot spot" with respect to the popularity of narcocorridos, not only because many are produced there, but also because they are very popular in clubs and on radio stations serving the near-majority Hispanic population.

Finally, I conducted interviews with members of a norteño group that performs all along the border and performs corridos (including narcocorridos) as an important part of their repertoire. These interviews were conducted in Douglas, Arizona, a small border town directly across from Agua Prieta in Mexico.

The research was therefore organized on the lines of what George Marcus (1998) has called "multi-site ethnographic research." It followed current theoretical developments in anthropology and other social sciences that seek to move beyond a strict construction of culture as tied to place. These developments are particularly relevant when studying cultural representations as they are produced, disseminated, and consumed via mass media, because mass-media representations flow so quickly across geographic space and are so easily available to be incorporated, adapted—or rejected—by people from a broad range of cultural traditions.

Social Stratification and Poverty on the Border

Thinking along the lines of multisited ethnography, however, does not mean ruling out any consideration of geography. The context of place still has a part to play in the meaning of representations; it just may not be the only or the final word. In this research, the geographic area in which most of the research took place retains some importance in understanding narcocorridos and the narco-trafficker image because the corrido genre at issue was born in a border context. Moreover, the area provides a historically relevant setting for assessing connections between social stratification and cultural representations. The U.S.-Mexico border is characterized by high poverty, migration, population flux, and a proliferation of cross-border factories, known as maquilas (or *maquiladoras*). The maquilas exemplify what has become the prevalent organization of labor among transnational corporations in the past several decades: administrative and technical operations located in the home country, with manufacturing or assembly located offshore, or across the border, where inexpensive labor can be found (see Sklair 1989; Dwyer 1994). There are well over three hundred such maquilas on the Mexican side of the border in Juárez. While the maquilas have created employment on both sides of the border (though the flow of wage labor, not surprisingly, has moved to the Mexican side), much of the employment is low wage and characterized by high turnover (Dwyer 1994). Poverty in many large border cities such as Juárez is rampant, and the colonias on its outskirts are filled with house-holds living in wood-and-scrap shacks and often headed by single women who work in the maquilas. More than 100,000 residents have no running water (see Moore 2000).

Even on the U.S. side of the border, the poverty rate is one-third greater than the national average, and per capita income is 12 per-cent below the average. Unemployment is high, and one-quarter of adults have less than a high school education (U.S. White House, Office of the Press Secretary, *Bulletin*, May 25, 1999). At the same time, the population is growing twice as fast as in the rest of the country and is much younger. In Juárez itself, only about one-quarter of the population has completed grade school (information from Juárez SISVEA [Sistema de Vigilancia Epidemiológica de las Adicciones—Epidemiologic Survey System of Addictions] director, Esteban Román Olvera, M.D., in Proceedings of Border Epidemi-ology Work Group, August 1998). And El Paso, despite its gleaming city center, is the poorest large city in Texas and the fourth poor-est in the country (U.S. Census Bureau, 1992), with 25 percent of families living below the poverty line. It is also approximately 73 percent Hispanic.

Finally, the reality of social stratification by racial or ethnic cate-gory in Mexico cannot be ignored. Despite the historical represen-tation of Mexican culture as mestizo, a deep racism born during the Spanish invasion and conquest remains as a "disdain for pure Indi-ans and a special respect for güeros, or whites" (Riding 1989, p. 7). Accompanying the racism is the socioeconomic fact that Indian peoples are, by and large, the poorest of Mexicans, while those of European (*criollo*) ancestry have traditionally been overrepresented among the economic elite, a pattern that mirrors the general legacy of European colonialism in the New World. Also not unusual is that the most egregious racism against Indian peoples is often reported as coming from mestizos (Riding 1989, pp. 199–218). Apropos this research, rural people—a large part of the narcocorrido audience—may in general be more associated with poverty and "Indian-ness."

Narcocorridos as Subject Matter

Examining narcocorridos and their social context and role provides an excellent vehicle for the examination of broader questions re-lated to the construction, production, and interpretation of media images and archetypes as they relate to poverty and social stratifi-cation, and the relationship between these media images and indi-vidual practice. This is so because narcocorridos are a current iteration of the corrido form, a very deeply rooted vehicle in Mexican culture for the representation and dissemination of culturally significant values and social roles. In their current form, however, they have melded into the larger domain of mass media. This, as will be argued, not only has transformed certain elements of their essential character, but also has changed the way in which they exert influence as purveyors of culturally shaped messages.

To begin understanding narcocorridos and the context in which they are produced and consumed, a brief background on corridos and narcocorridos follows.

Corridos and the U.S.-Mexico Border as Contested Terrain

While most scholars of Mexican folklore agree that the corrido has its roots in the Spanish romance ballads brought over by soldiers during and after the conquest, there is some divergence regarding the degree to which they were reborn in the New World as a northern border or a Mexico-wide phenomenon (see Herrera-Sobek 1993, on the general divergence of views between Vicente Mendoza and Merle Simmons and Américo Paredes with respect to this issue). In this book, I do not intend, nor do I have the expertise, to resolve this question. It is not, in any case, vital for this work (and would be an unnecessary diversion), since many of the thematic issues remain similar whether corridos have a border-area or broader origin, and because narcocorridos have now become popularized across Mexico and among other Mexican and Hispanic populations. Suffice it to say that the evidence of which I am aware appears to substantially support the argument for corridos as a border phenomenon; therefore, I will work from that position. It is worth noting that narcocorrido and corrido groups are typically seen as producing norteño music, and many of the famous (and not so famous) narcocorrido groups are either from the border area or at least identify themselves as musicians from the northern part of Mexico (e.g., Los Huracanes del Norte, Los Tigres del Norte, Los Dinámicos del Norte, El Poder del Norte, and several groups from Tijuana). This is not to say that corridos are not produced elsewhere: McDowell (2000), for example, documents a rich tradition of heroic and violent corridos in Mexico's Costa Chica region, where the Sierra Madre del Sur touches the Pacific Ocean.

As so well described by Paredes (1958, 1978, 1993) and Martínez (1988, 1994), the Texas border region, framed by the Rio Grande, was, from the early days of Spanish colonization on the North American continent, "inhabited by outlaws, whose principal offense was an independent spirit" (Paredes 1958, p. 8). It was an empty spot of sorts, between other, more prominent, areas of Spanish colonization in New Mexico and farther north in what is now Texas. Even after the area was settled by Spanish colonists, it retained a sense of isolation; outsiders from both Central Mexico (*fuereños*) and the north (gringos) were viewed as "foreigners" (Paredes 1958, 1993). While El Paso lies to the northwest of the area central to Paredes' work, and while El Paso was colonized earlier (El Paso del Norte was an important stop on the passage north to what is now New Mexico), many of the same cultural characteristics apply. Both border areas evolved as unified settlements that transcended sides of the river-cum-border, and most of these areas evolved a cultural tradition of independence from the governmental center (Martínez 1988). They also have a tradition of being regarded as trouble zones.

Following the Mexican-American War and the Treaty of Guadalupe Hidalgo (signed in 1848), a border was imposed upon a once-unified region. Subsequently, as a contact zone between countries, the South Texas border has been "fundamentally heterogeneous, defined by forces of social differentiation—ethnicity, class, language, power. . . . Historically, the tenor of the contact, its dominant relational temper, has been one of conflict, engendered by the enforced domination of Anglos over a subject people" (Bauman 1993, p. xiii). Some of the tenor of conflict can also be attributed to the existence of a border per se, which by nature (for any border) is a liminal zone and thus an area in which the potential loss of sociocultural control is great. The potential for loss is perhaps even greater for the dominant party, which may believe itself to have the most to lose. The perceived threat generates a felt need for control (manifested as state control).

In any case, the ensuing struggle for border-area Mexicans to establish an identity in an environment of conflict has included the evolution of the corrido. Since that time, the popularity of the corrido, and the subject matter addressed, have ebbed and flowed with the nature and intensity of cross-border tensions, whether these are focused on immigration issues or smuggling or the ubiquitous drug trade and (now) the looming presence of cartels affiliated with that trade. To this general scenario we may also add the rapid growth of the maquilas, as described above, and the resulting strain placed on all social and economic systems to support the large influx of people from other regions in Mexico who have flocked to the border to find work and who, for the most part, live in the ever-expanding colonias.

The Emergence and Role of the Corrido

As a form of narrative discourse, corridos in general are historical narratives that focus on "events of particular consequence to
the corrido community . . . selecting events for narration which
have instrumental and symbolic value in the corrido community"
(McDowell 1981, p. 46).[3] The events are usually (though not always)
presented by an impersonal voice not involved in the events portrayed. Significantly, McDowell (1981) notes the incomplete nature
of corridos, arguing that as a form of information they presuppose a
community already informed about the events narrated; thus they
are not a form of "folk news." As Herrera-Sobek (1979, p. 49) has
noted, "careful examination of the Mexican corrido or Mexican
folksong yields valuable information as to the ideology, world view,
political, economic, and social situation of the Mexican people."

The type of corrido that is the historical antecedent of the narcocorrido celebrates "the defiant and heroic exploits of Gregorio Cortez and Jacinto Treviño, the *sediciosos* [seditions] of Aniceto Pizaña,
and even the *tequilero* smugglers [tequila smugglers] of the border . . . [providing a] ground on which to reject the imputation of
fatalistic accommodation" (Bauman 1993, p. xv). Corridos as a whole
have included other themes as well, such as immigration; migrant
labor; working conditions on the railroads, in the fields, and under
the *bracero* program; love lost when migrating to the United States;
and other issues—including conflict with the central government
in Mexico (Herrera-Sobek 1990, 1993). They are also closely related
to other border music forms (McDowell 1981; Paredes 1976). The corridos of focus here, however, are those known as *corridos trágicos*,
primarily corridos about heroes (McDowell 1981; Mendoza 1964;
Paredes 1958). These corridos come most recently from the Rio
Grande area beginning in the mid-nineteenth century, growing out
of the increasing conflict between the long-time border inhabitants
of Spanish-Indian heritage and the encroaching Anglo Texans.

It could also be said that this distinct genre of early corridos developed as the obverse of an emerging, and racist, body of Texas
folklore portraying Mexicans as cruel, thieving, cowardly, "racially
degenerate" half-breeds with Indian blood, and generally no match
for the superior Texan, as exemplified by the Texas Ranger archetype (Paredes 1958, 1978). These corridos told of exploits against the
"*rinches*" (Rangers), mocked them, and generally treated them as
an Anglo stereotype exemplifying the general nature of the cultural
and political opposition. It is important to note that corridos arose
from a common and "generally favorable disposition" toward indi-

viduals who disregarded the imposed legalities of a border (i.e., customs, immigration, etc.) and treated the land on both sides of the river as home, as one place. In this sense, the smugglers, illegal immigrants, and outlaws have been viewed as an outgrowth of a shared social situation (Paredes 1978). Thus corrido heroes follow the pattern of "social banditry" described by Hobsbawm (1969).

According to Arturo Ramírez (1990, p. 72), the heart of the relationship between the corrido hero and the world around him is the "confrontation between the hero and hostile Anglo-American forces." Citing José Saldívar (1986, p. 12), Ramírez writes that the paradigm of this type of corrido has three basic components:

1. A charismatic and heroic protagonist, "with whom the Chicano or Mexican audience is presumed to identify in some way";
2. The world as viewed by the Chicano audience, a world dominated by "antagonistic, often Anglo-American forces," with whom the hero must contend; and
3. "Oral narrative, in which the interaction of the protagonist and the world is described."

As event, traditional corridos were performed alone by solitary male singers at family gatherings and in the cantina or on a *parranda* (typically for an all-male audience) (according to Paredes 1976, cited in McDowell 1981).[4] One corrido often held out as a model for the heroic genre is "El Corrido de Gregorio Cortez." According to the legend (Paredes 1958), Gregorio Cortez was a well-known *vaquero* (Mexican ranch hand, prototype for the American cowboy), from the border area between South Texas and Mexico. He was said to be the best there was, as a vaquero, as a farmer, and as a man—unfailingly polite, respectful, while at the same time brave and a superb shot. It is said that, while in Texas, Gregorio's brother was falsely accused of stealing a horse and that he was shot and killed by the sheriff who came to arrest him. The sheriff then turned to shoot Gregorio, who shot him first. Eventually, after a long chase, he turned himself in and was jailed. Throughout the story, though, Gregorio Cortez is held in high esteem by his own nationals and eventually by some Americans as well, who know that they have in him a formidable yet honorable foe. Thus the following corrido (slightly modified from the Arhoolie Records translation):

El Corrido de Gregorio Cortez
In the county of El Carmen
look what has happened

The major sheriff died
leaving Román wounded.

The following morning,
when the people arrived,
some told the others
they don't know who killed him.

They were investigating,
and about three hours later,
they found out that the wrongdoer
was Gregorio Cortez.

Cortez was wanted
throughout the state
Alive or dead may he be apprehended,
for he has killed several.

Said Gregorio Cortez
with his pistol in his hand,
"I'm not sorry for having killed him.
It's for my brother that I feel sorry."

Said Gregorio Cortez
with his soul aflame,
"I'm not sorry for having killed him,
self-defense is permitted."

The Americans came.
They flew like the wind
because they were going to win
the three thousand–dollar reward.

He continued toward Gonzales
Several sheriffs saw him.
They did not want to follow
because they were afraid of him.

The hound dogs came,
they came on his trail.
But to reach Cortez
was like reaching a star.

Gregorio Cortez said,
"What's the use of plans
if you can't catch me
even with those hound dogs."

The Americans said,
"If we see him, what shall we do to him?
If we face him head on,
very few will return."

In the ranch corral
they managed to surround him,
a few more than 300 men,
and there he gave them the slip.

There around Encinal,
from all that they say,
they had a shoot-out,
and he killed another sheriff.

Gregorio Cortez said,
with his pistol in his hand,
"Don't run, you cowardly Rangers,
from one lone Mexican."

He turned toward Laredo
without a single fear,
"Follow me, you cowardly Rangers,
I am Gregorio Cortez."

Gregorio says to Juan
at the Cypress Ranch,
"Tell me what's new,
I am Gregorio Cortez."

Gregorio says to Juan,
"Very soon you will see,
go and tell the sheriffs
that they should come and arrest me."

When the sheriffs arrived,
Gregorio presented himself,
"You'll take me if I wish it,
because there is no other way."

Now they caught Cortez,
now the case is closed;
his poor family
he carries in his heart.

Now with this I take my leave
in the shade of the cypress.

Here we finish singing
the tragedy of Cortez.[5]

Another prototypical corrido, or set of corridos, is about the
famed (and, some say, imaginary) Joaquín Murieta (Herrera-Sobek
1993; Sonnichsen 1975). As legend has it, Murieta turned to a life
of banditry after his wife and brother were abducted and killed by
Americans in a California mining town. The Murieta corridos detail
the history of a classic social bandit. The following is one version:

Joaquín Murieta
I am not an American
But I do understand English.
I learned it with my brother
Forward and backward
And any American
I make tremble at my feet.

When I was barely a child
I was left an orphan.
No one gave me any love,
They killed my brother,
And my wife Carmelita,
The cowards assassinated her.

I came from Hermosillo
In search of gold and riches.
The Indian poor and simple
I defended with fierceness
And a good price the sheriffs
Would pay for my head.

From the greedy rich,
I took away their money.
With the humble and poor
I took off my hat.
Oh, what unjust laws
To call me a highwayman.

Murieta does not like
To be falsely accused.
I come to avenge my wife,
And again I repeat it,
Carmelita so lovely
How they made her suffer.

Through bars I went
Punishing Americans.
"You must be the captain
Who killed my brother.
You grabbed him defenseless
You stuck-up American."

My career began
Because of a terrible scene.
When I got to seven hundred (killed)
Then my name was dreaded,
When I got to twelve hundred
Then my name was terrible.

I am the one who dominates
Even African lions.
That's why I go out on the road
To kill Americans.
Now my destiny is no other,
Watch out, you people!

Pistols and daggers
Are playthings for me.
Bullets and stabbings
Big laughs for me.
With their means cut off
They're afraid around here.

I'm neither a Chilean nor a stranger
On this soil which I tread.
From Mexico to California
Because God wanted it that way,
And in my stitched serape,
I carry my baptismal birth certificate.

How pretty is California
With her well laid-out streets,
Where Murieta passed by
With his troops,
With his loaded pistol,
And his silver-plated saddle.

I've had a good time in California
Through the year of '50
With my silver-plated saddle
And my pistol loaded

I am that Mexican
By the name of Joaquín Murieta.[6]

As can be seen, the verses chronicle Murieta's reaction to injustice, including the following angry words: "Through bars I went / Punishing Americans / 'You must be the captain / Who killed my brother / You grabbed him defenseless / You stuck-up American.' " Or boastful words: "Pistols and daggers / Are playthings for me / Bullets and stabbings / Big laughs for me / With their means cut off / They're afraid around here." And there are clearly lines that specifically characterize Murieta as a "social bandit": "I came from Hermosillo / In search of gold and riches / The Indian poor and simple / I defended with fierceness . . . / From the greedy rich / I took away their money / With the humble and poor / I took off my hat / Oh, what unjust laws / To call me a highwayman." Many of these stylistic forms also appear in narcocorridos, as noted later.[7]

In addition to, or as a subset of, the genre of corridos just described, there has been a tradition of corridos that focus on the theme of smuggling. It is this historical genre that narcocorridos most closely follow. Herrera-Sobek (1979) refers to a few examples of older corridos (e.g., "Mariano Reséndez," "Los Tequileros," "Dionisio Maldonado," "El Contrabando de El Paso") about smugglers of various sorts. Mariano Reséndez, as an example, apparently was a popular textile smuggler viewed as a folk hero who was apprehended and killed by supporters of the regime of Porfirio Díaz near the turn of the century. Corrido lyrics portray him as a man who was brave and courageous (not afraid of bullets), who provided food for the people, and who thought of his mother (see also Paredes 1976). During Prohibition (1920s–1930s), numerous corridos were written about liquor smugglers, or "tequileros." Very much like the drug smugglers of more recent times, the tequileros were sometimes apprehended by the U.S. Border Patrol, and sometimes did battle with them. In fact, as can be seen in the following example of a classic smuggler corrido, the themes of treachery and betrayal are common, very much as in the later narcocorridos:

Contrabandistas Tequileros
In 1930, gentlemen,
your attention, please.
In the jail of Del Rio
this song was made into poetry.

I would rather not remember
the Del Rio jail,

where on the seventeenth of March
they were going to sentence us.

They took us out of the jail
straight to the Calle Real,
and the Colorado told us
that he was going to take our pictures.

After they had taken our pictures,
they took us to the jail,
and we didn't know our sentence,
because they didn't explain it to us.

A pretty jail in Del Rio,
but it doesn't console me,
because they give us plain beans
and a little plate of oatmeal.

A pretty jail in Del Rio,
but it's still unbelievable.
You can count the friends
who want to go see you.

I tell my friends
when they're going to cross [the river],
Watch out for the informers,
that they don't turn you in.

I tell my friends
when they're on the other side,
Be careful on the trails
where the Colorado passes.

Perhaps in Naqueví
they have already caught a comrade
who sold liquor to an informer
on the thirtieth day of January.

Watch it, informer,
because I am saying,
that for the love of money,
you were selling us out.

But that no longer matters;
neither must one think about it.
We're going to drink some beer
and later mess around.

But that no longer matters,
what has happened is over.
Because of an informer
I find myself a prisoner here.

I went on many sprees
with friends in good cars,
and today they take me prisoner
with no one to bring me a cigarette.

Don't cry, Mama,
I carry you in my heart.
For bringing in contraband,
Prohibition agents have taken me.

Understand, my friends,
and take much care.
For going around selling drink,
they're taking us to Leavenworth.

The Southern Pacific engine
runs violently,
and it takes the convicts
straight to the penitentiary.

These verses were made
by everyone together,
some because of contraband
and others because of immigration.

Good-bye, my dear mother,
only you cry for my troubles.
They are taking us prisoners,
joined together with a chain.

Good-bye, my dear mother,
I'm going to the penitentiary.
When I get out, we'll see each other,
God willing.

Good-bye, Del Rio jail,
good-bye, towers and bells,
good-bye all my friends,
good-bye, beautiful Mexican girls.

Those who live in Del Rio
are tranquil,

because they drink
tequila easily.

Now with this [verse] I say good-bye
because I'm feeling very cold,
and here we are finished singing
of the contraband of Del Rio.[8]

Note that this corrido is not so much the tale of a specific, known person, but of a common circumstance that befell smugglers, told as the story of what happened to an anonymous individual. It is, as is evident, also an extended "lament" regarding the situation the convict finds himself in.

I include a second smuggler corrido because this one, "Corrido de los Bootleggers," contains other themes that occur in some narco-corridos concerning the relationship between smuggling and social conditions (Arhoolie Records translation):

Corrido de los Bootleggers
Be careful, gentlemen,
of what I will sing for you here.
I raffled my luck
with fourteen federal men.

I began thinking, gentlemen,
that there was no more work.
I had to make a living,
God willing.

The crops are not good,
I have nothing else to say.
Now the best crop
is the one from the barrels.

Everyone who plants
must wait until next year.
Now is it not the barrels,
once the first one comes out.

Those who cook the liquor
to no one do they wish evil,
but they are turned in
and they bring in the federal agents.

When delivering the liquor,
with danger, although it is cheap,

I just take two or three drinks,
and my fear doesn't last long.

As long as the bars remain,
it will always be like this,
because the poor are in jail
and the rich are having a good time.

But the son never pays attention,
before he has been caught.
The mother is the one who suffers
when her son is locked up.

You will find my mother sad,
and my father with more reason,
to see their son locked up
in this sad prison.

Oh, my poor mother,
what luck she has had.
At the doors of this jail
she has shed tears.

My mother very eagerly
talks with the lawyer,
to see if she can get me out on bail
from the county jail.

I was a successful bootlegger
because I had never been caught,
because all of my deliveries
were made carefully.

Here in San Antonio,
and its surroundings,
they never catch the bootleggers,
only those who work for them.

When we got there,
they told me right away,
"Here in this penitentiary
you are sentenced even if not guilty."

He who made these verses
is not a noteworthy composer.
In the center of this record [is]
the name by which he is known.

This is the farewell,
don't get me wrong.
Be careful with the barrels because
the federal officials might get you.[9]

Note that the third stanza clearly represents a basic, pragmatic rationale for involvement in smuggling that could be applied today, not only in Mexico but in Colombia and many other parts of the world. In the seventh stanza, there is also a clear statement about the hypocrisy involved in the unequal position of the liquor provider, who is cast as smuggler, versus the consumer, who is simply "having a good time": "As long as the bars remain / it will always be like this / because the poor are in jail / and the rich are having a good time." As will be seen, this sentiment is common in narcocorridos and among the narcocorrido community.

The Corrido as a "Marked" Genre

Given all that has just been said about themes common to corridos, it must also be acknowledged that their themes and affective character exist in part because it is a genre marked for these themes and sentiments. As such, there is an element of selectivity in terms of content. McDowell (1981) and Paredes (1976) clearly demonstrate this in several examples, including the corridos about Gregorio Cortez, which concentrate exclusively on his confrontation and bravery vis-à-vis the Texas Rangers and the tragedy that prompted his actions. In the full story, there was a series of trials, after which Cortez was in fact acquitted. As McDowell (1981, pp. 50–51) notes:

> The corrido is propositional in the broadest sense, asserting a collective sense of identity by incorporating signs and symbols which have special resonance in the corrido community. The propositional character of the corrido is implemented through several devices, all of which interact to reinforce a common cosmological orientation. To begin with, the corrido's very selection of events worthy of narration proceeds from a notably ethnocentric bias. The corrido seeks out moments of active, violent confrontation, in which death to either or both parties is a distinct and immediate possibility. . . . The events selected for narration in the corrido answer to community values and orientations.

This applies to some degree to the actual terms and objects that have a presence in the narration, which may entail the use of terms like "*pistola*" or "corral," or other terms that refer to objects familiar in the corrido community. This, as will be noted later, has interesting implications with respect to narcocorridos.

Moreover, McDowell, in his later exegesis of the corridos of Costa Chica (2000), proposes that the corrido is deeply and symbolically intertwined with the practice of violence in the community, serving three discursive tasks: celebrating, regulating, and then healing the violence. The corrido itself is thus a key component of the ongoing cycle of violence.

The Emergence, Thematic Content, and Distribution Mode of Narcocorridos

Beginning in the 1960s and the 1970s, however, corridos began to appear that evidenced a new twist on the older smuggling theme. These new corridos were about drug smugglers or traffickers. Herrera-Sobek (1979) mentions several of these, and Paredes (1978) also refers to nearly a dozen corridos inspired by the death of a trafficker named Juan Carrasco in 1976, who was widely believed to have been "executed" at close range by a Texas Ranger. Also in the 1970s, Los Tigres del Norte—a group that continues to perform and is one of the most famous norteño bands—sang corridos such as "Contrabando y Traición" (Contraband and Betrayal) and "Camelia la Tejana"—the latter about a woman (unusual, especially in the 1970s) who was a popular figure in her community and who became a drug smuggler. Both Herrera-Sobek and Paredes, however, contend that these early "narcocorridos" reflect the community's strong moral stance against drug smuggling, along with a certain sadness about the almost inevitable consequences of a life in that world. In addition, Paredes (1978) argues that the drug smuggler does not inspire the same sense of admiration that the old corrido heroes did. Herrera-Sobek (1979, p. 53) argues this case as well, even though, as she notes, many of these corridos "extol the daring, the cunning, the clever maneuvering of the smuggler (because the corridista's common sense and sensitivity makes him aware that no man is all good or all bad)." Yet Paredes' and Herrera-Sobek's initial views may no longer fully reflect the currency, popularity, and more recent blossoming of this genre in conjunction with a number of factors, including current social circumstances that exist in conjunction with the drug-trafficking industry in Mexico. These factors include, for example, the economic crisis surrounding devaluation of the peso, NAFTA, and various issues related to the maquila industries, frictions, and problems surrounding immigration and drug-interdiction efforts; the mass marketing of these narcocorridos; the increasing prominence and market power of the Hispanic community throughout the United States; and the cross-referencing of images with rap, hip-hop, and so-called gangsta rap. Their views also predate the rise and media coverage of major narcotraffickers such as Caro Quintero in the 1980s, and, more recently, Amado Carillo Fuentes (of the Juárez cartel) and Arellano Félix (the Tijuana cartel). Some of these figures have, at one point or another, acted the part of the "social bandit." In any case, the new corridos, according to one source (Quiñones 1998, p. G1) "celebrate shootouts with *federales,* betrayals and executions and stories of how legendary [drug] traffickers fell and how cargoes got through." It is these narcocorridos which are the subject of this research.

The genre as it is known today grew dramatically following the popularity of corridos written and recorded in the late 1980s by a Mexican migrant named Rosalino Sánchez, better known as "Chalino" (Quiñones 1998).[10] These were picked up by small studios and the Spanish-language record industry in and around Los Angeles, which has become the recording center for narcocorridos, even though they are essentially a Mexican product. They are now found along the border, in Mexico, in cities of the Southwest, and elsewhere where there is a high percentage of Mexican Americans (and Mexican migrants). Moreover, recordings by some of the better-known groups can typically be found anyplace in the United States where there is a significant Mexican or Central American population. As the progenitor of the genre, Chalino's voice was said to be rough, heavy with an accent from his home state of Sinaloa on the Pacific coast of Mexico—at odds with the usual polished quality of Mexican pop stars, but qualities that enormously strengthened his appeal as a singer of the common people (Quiñones 1998). The wave of narcocorrido singers who have followed Chalino emulate his Sinaloan speech and dress style, which in turn has had a widespread effect on Mexican American youth style—a sort of "Sinaloan narcotraficante chic." He remains an "authentic folk hero," even though he was killed in 1992 (Quiñones 2001a, p. 12).

Furthermore, marketing and presentation of the narcocorridos appear to draw from rap and hip-hop, possibly because many of the Mexican and Mexican American youth who listen to them grew up with rap. Consequently, an intense debate has arisen about their effect, particularly on younger listeners. Many radio stations in Mexico and in the southwestern United States do not play the narcocorridos, in any case, and in a number of cities, including El Paso/Ciudad Juárez (primary site of this research), officials have specifically asked radio stations not to play them (Quiñones 2001a).

They are, however, widely available on audiotapes and CDs, and many Mexican norteño, pop, and folk bands that are not "narco-corrido bands" are often asked to play them (according to conversations I have had with norteño musicians). The appeal is apparently strong: "For many immigrants," notes Quiñones (1998, p. G8), "the corridos prove that someone has made something of themselves in America."

In contrast to the performance settings for traditional corridos, there is a marked change. Narcocorridos are "performed" both live and electronically on tapes and CDs. Live performances occur at nightclubs, festivals, concerts, and other events, as well as in cantinas and in some of the more traditional settings. In recorded or broadcast form, the performances may be in a car, in someone's house, outside while working, at a gathering of some kind, or in any other setting where tape or CD players or a radio is present. Thus the nature of performance is, for the most part, much different from that of the classic corrido.

Preliminary fieldwork conducted in the Juárez/El Paso area at the beginning of the research period suggested several general factors to consider in an attempt to understand the sociohistorical context against which the narcotrafficker image is given meaning:

1. A common, and historically continuous, undercurrent of antagonism on the border that colors Anglo and Mexican perceptions of each other and of particular situations, regardless of the actual nature of events. It is a negative sentiment, a certain resistance to those things that are viewed as symbols of American encroachment and domination, whether these are represented as the maquila industries (and the wealth they represent) or the ubiquitous presence of the border patrol, or the encroachment of American cultural values and practices. This undercurrent, however, is ambiguous and situational and exists simultaneously with desires for certain aspects of American life—particularly the material;
2. The class system in Mexico itself, which, to a large extent, remains ethnically based (European, mestizo, Indian);
3. The long history of drug cultivation and trafficking in northern Mexico and its integration into cultural patterns. Traffickers are said to be the primary source, in some small and rural communities, of economic development, new schools, and other such benefits. Moreover, the business of trafficking is often conducted by families; and

4. The poverty and large colonias that exist amidst the
   ostensible economic boon of the maquilas.

Against these factors, it appeared likely that the narcotrafficker
was commonly viewed by non-elite Mexicans as a "social bandit,"
as a symbol of power and efficacy outside the domination of the
United States or of the Mexican elite, in short, as a model for how
to be a person of status and importance even in the face of subordinate social position—a model, one could say, of social mobility.
In this sense, I considered the possible similarity in process and
content between narcotraffickers and other "outlaw personas" that
have evolved in analogous situations of long-term social disparity,
though such personas will be shaped in symbolic content by the social and cultural factors present in their particular situations. They
will present themselves, and be interpreted or represented by community members, according to a symbolic code that has evolved
from the situation. They are personas or cultural archetypes within
that code—which, in the tradition of the bricoleur, is likely to incorporate elements from local, culturally specific discourses, and
now (due to the influence of the mass media in particular), trans-
national/transcultural discourses. Moreover, and important for this
research, I sought to consider potential similarities in the specific
behavior patterns that are characteristic of such outlaw personas.

The methodology used for the research is discussed in Appendix I.

3. Interpreting Narcocorridos

Following the research plan (see Appendix 1), I collected interview and observation data in several domains, and I will report it here in a similar format: a brief narrative analysis of a sample of narcocorridos; listener interpretations; social context; the impact of mass media market on the nature of these corridos; and connections between the narcocorrido persona and personal action (i.e., practice). In Chapter 4 I shall discuss and synthesize the role of the narco-trafficker persona as a cultural figure, the social context in which that figure gains resonance, and a number of propositions about the role of such "cultural personas" in general and their connections to individual action.

Narcocorrido texts discussed in this chapter are from a sample of those that I translated or was able to have translated from a collection of tapes and CDs I obtained during fieldwork in Juárez/El Paso and Tijuana, and in Los Angeles. I found them almost anywhere tapes and CDs were sold. But they were also very common in the jukeboxes, or *rocolas,* that are found in almost every cantina. The narcocorridos that I translated are only a small representation of the number that exist or are recorded and distributed, but they include several that are commonly known, as well as others that were recommended by various individuals with whom I worked, including norteño musicians.

Narcocorridos as Corridos

What is the relationship between narcocorridos and traditional or classic corridos? This is important because, if we assume that narcocorridos are interpreted in some way as corridos, some commonalities of form and tone are likely. To define this relationship, we can look at similarity of form and similarity of content. I am less concerned with detailed analysis of form, because it is my experience that listeners understand something to be a corrido not based primarily on a strict judgment of form, but on a very general sense of form and sound, combined with content. Moreover, a number of the early but notable "border conflict" or border hero songs discussed by Paredes (1976) appear in forms related to the corrido, such as the *copla* or *décima.* Some comments on this subject, however, are pertinent. McDowell (1972) has set out a general structure for corridos: (a) introductory reference to performance; (b) setting: place, date, and name of principals; (c) core—verbal exchange or expression, interspersed with narrative detail; (d) farewell of principal; and (e) *despedida,* closing reference to performance. So, for example, the Corrido de Inés Chávez García (see García Torres 1997; V. T. Mendoza 1944), begins with this reference to performance:

> Gentlemen, I present to you
> what happened in Peribán:
> there was a bloody battle;
> [Rafael]Nares ("el mocho") died.

This is followed by the body of the text describing the actual incident, which, in turn, is followed by a farewell and the close of the performance:

> And with this I say good-bye
> at the edge of town.
> Here I finish singing
> the verses of Peribán.

I did not often find this form present in this clear and formal manner in the narcocorridos I encountered. In fact, as will be seen, many narcocorridos close with a warning of some kind: to those who would try and "get" the protagonist, about the treachery involved in the business, or about the tragic consequences of mixing romance with the world of drug trafficking. This represents a contrast with classic corridos such as those discussed earlier. In those, the introductory reference and despedida are more clearly present, though in "Corrido de los Bootleggers," the despedida is combined with a warning.

There are other contrasts. For one, classic corridos tend to be much longer than narcocorridos and more drawn out and lamenting in style, with references to the suffering of mothers whose sons have been jailed, to the loss of friends, or to sorrow and loneliness upon being taken from home (to the penitentiary). I attribute this in part to the fact that classic corridos are in an oral and not yet mass media format. Narcocorridos, on the other hand, are in part molded by the requirements of the popular-song format, in which "short" and "punchy" are key values. Nevertheless, people commonly understand narcocorridos to be corridos, primarily because of the general sound and narrative content.

I should note here that there is one narrative or stylistic element characteristic of many classic corridos that is also present in narcocorridos, but that does not come through in the translations. I refer here to the poetic element of the lyrics, which, when sung, build on the rhythmic cadence of the music. For example, in the well-known narcocorrido "Contrabando y Traición," there is the following verse in Spanish:

> Sonaron siete balazos, Camelia a Emilio mataba
> La policía solo halló una pistola tirada
> Del dinero y Camelia, nunca más se supo nada

Yet in English this is translated as

> Seven gunshots were heard; Camelia killed Emilio
> A gun thrown on the ground was all the police found
> No one heard anything again, of the money or Camelia

This is important to acknowledge, because the English translations that appear in the description and analysis that follow lose this element of poetics, of performance. We can, however, focus on the narrative content and stipulate that, when performed, corridos and narcocorridos appeal for reasons of poetics as well. (The Spanish versions of all corridos in this text appear in Appendix 2.) Even though, as McDowell (1981) notes, word choice may be influenced by the desire to create rhyme and poetic sensibility, I would argue that this does not materially affect the narrative content, because the content is more global in character and—as noted earlier—central to a listener's understanding that a particular song is a corrido.

The following narcocorridos are just a few illustrative selections, translated into English with commentary.[1] The groups represented in this sample are among the best known. The first narcocorrido, "El Tarasco," shows some of the "boasting" tonality of many narcocorridos—also a characteristic of classic corridos. In "El Tarasco," the boasting is about the narcotrafficker's (and, in this case, also the corridista's) ability to defy the authorities' attempts to capture him or hold him in jail. It is also a boast, or a boost, for the narrator's home state, Michoacán—"I'm not [superhuman], but I am from Michoacán." The manner of the boast is measured, more along the lines of an affirmation of identity: "I'm not superhuman," but even though I'm not, I am, in effect, "who I am" (I am from Michoacán). The boasting, as will be seen, also refers to the beauty of the land in Michoacán, a reminder that the whole process of growing and distributing drugs is also intertwined with a rural consciousness, a tie to the land and a sense of autonomy vis-à-vis the central government. Thus it is also an affirmation of local identity and rural identity.

There is, as well, in this corrido an angry poke at duplicitous government officials who, one moment, sanction the trafficker's activity and benefit from it, but in the next moment, they bring it down or arrest the same trafficker for expediency's sake. This is a common aspect of the world of narcotrafficking, a world in which the lines between legitimate and illegitimate activity are blurred and shifting. Indeed, the infamous trafficker Pablo Acosta routinely carried official Mexican government identification for use as necessary, and he even cooperated on occasion with American law enforcement officials (see Poppa 1990).

Finally, the last stanzas contain a theme common to many narcocorridos: betrayal by informants or others, even by those who were believed to be close or intimate. In this corrido, however, there is little reference to what might be called greater social themes of justice, which are integral to some of the classic corridos.

El Tarasco

First, they gave me wings [they let me fly high],
and now they want to stop me [to ground me].
I'm not a toy monkey
that you can wind up whenever you want.
I'm not Juan Colorado [I'm not superhuman],
But I am from Michoacán.

How much could the mountain range
from Michoacán to Colima cost?
I am forever coveting
[the land around] the creek at Aguilillas.
There the fighting cocks are fine
and the girls pretty

Do not waste any more money on buying more radars
or on destroying my landing strips,
[because] I'm a nocturnal bird

that can land in any cornfield.
Besides, the day I fall,
many others in high places [in high government positions] will
   also fall.

They freed me from jail
because it was convenient for them.
I was too much of a burden,
so they erased my name from the list.
When I return from Redwood City
I will make them pay for what they did.

Because of some rat fink [snitch]
I had a fall in Uruapán.
Also, my beloved Blondie-girl
betrayed me over there in Sahuayo.
Since I'm an honorable Tarasco
I will soon give them what they deserve.

Do not waste any more money on buying more radars
or on destroying my landing strips,
[because] I'm a nocturnal bird
that can land in any cornfield.
Besides, the day I fall,
many other more powerful ones will also fall with me.
(Performed by Los Tigres del Norte)

Note the similarity in themes between "El Tarasco" and the next narcocorrido, "Los Tres de la Sierra" (The Three Men of the Sierra). In this narcocorrido, there is also a certain regional pride expressed, as a personalized relationship to the land ("the ground gave to him") as well as both a fraternal and a paternal sentiment about the "good and courageous men" who are the subject of the lyrics, and the well-honed and successful businesses (money, new trucks) over which they preside. Two other common references also present in "Los Tres de la Sierra" are a level of resentment at Americans who are the consumers, but who devalue or criminalize the producers; and the ubiquitous entanglement of law and government officials in the business:

Los Tres de la Sierra
You see, my blond one, I picked up all the men
one stormy night on a pathway [gap] in the mountains.
Kiko was taking his people to pick the crops,
to gather the green gold that this year the earth gave him.

Armando drove the truck, a brand new Ram.
You damned Americans don't know what we go through
to get you the drugs you like so much.

Rubén says with a smile, "Look, we're almost there."
He warmed the engine while the men loaded the trunk.
It didn't matter that they were covered in mud and water
because they were well armed.

How pretty is the greenery at the foot of the mountains,
but even more beautiful are the packages of dollars when they
    arrive,
as Kiko happily pays out, to the law and to his men.

The three from the mountains can be seen in their new trucks.
On the border we see them watching over their business,
while on the ranch in the mountains the crops are growing.

There is no other [ranch] in the Sierra that has a name
    [reputation] like this one.
Francisco, Rubén, and Armando are moving out their men.
They are waiting for them anxiously, with courageous and
    quick men.
(Performed by Los Norteños de Ojinaga)

In "El General," the tone is not boastful; it tells a story about events that have befallen several individuals who are narcotraffickers or affiliated with them (and who even wanted to apprehend them). It is not even particularly pro-narcotrafficker, though it is sympathetic and assumes, in the last stanzas, a political stance about U.S.-Mexico drug politics that is very common in Mexico: there is a large dose of hypocrisy in U.S. policy, because the United States is the major source of demand, and because the "certification" process is so obviously political. According to one report, "El General" is primarily about Gen. Jesús Gutiérrez Rebollo, Mexican contact for the U.S. Drug Enforcement Administration (DEA), who was dismissed after being accused of being in the pay of Juárez cartel head Amado Carillo Fuentes (Wald 1998).

El General
A general has fallen,
the television said
When they gave him the job
they thought he was the best,

but because of his ties to narcotrafficking,
he now sits in prison.

They asked him for protection
in Culiacán and Jalisco.
They offered him good things.
The press said so.
He was living high on the hog,
and so the authorities started an investigation into his affairs.

Those large drug shipments
will no longer pass on through.
The one who made that possible
is now in jail,
and it has been reported that in Baja California
another general has fallen.

According to the statement
the general gave to the police,
he said he had always dreamed of
capturing "the lord of the skies,"[2]
and that was the reason he had befriended him:
in order to win his trust.

Not even with a million dollars
could the narcotraffickers bribe
the delegate in Tijuana,
that brave federal
There are people who love their job
and so care for it very well.

Different countries are certified by the Americans.
They don't want drugs to exist.
They say drugs are dangerous.
But tell me, who certifies
the United States?

Mexico has tried honestly and hard
to apprehend the narcotraffickers.
The Americans buy the cocaine.
They'll pay any price for it.
They say they don't want drugs to exist,
but [when it comes to certification]
they give themselves a big break.
(Performed by Los Tigres del Norte)

"Jesus Amado," in the manner of a classic corrido, is about a gun-fight between one brave individual and the police or authorities. It is not presented, at least on the surface, as a fight that represents a stand against some injustice. However, when understood in the context of self-identification as "bandits" (narcotraffickers), where bandits are "good and courageous men" in contrast to an "othered" identity of authority, whether Mexican or American, then there is a kind of injustice involved: the tragedy of good men taken down either by weaker, less-proud, less-independent government func-tionaries or through treachery, betrayal, jealousy, or other malfea-sance. Treachery is also part of the story of "Jesus Amado" and is a common narcocorrido twist in which the subject shifts to betrayal.

Jesús Amado
Jiménez is his last name,
His first name Jesús Amado.
He fought the Brownsville police
on the shores of the Río Bravo,
but they weren't able to take away his cargo
because he's a fighting cock.

At about 11:00 A.M.
someone made a call
saying that Amado always crossed his load in an inner tube,
that he would cross at 2:00 A.M.

A searchlight spotted him,
and several shots rang out.
Amado fired back
with his "Perki" and an AK-47,
killing two policemen.
The other five ran away.

When he returned to Sinaloa,
he put a price on the snitch's head,
but he was very surprised when they told him
that his woman had betrayed him.

When he went to confront her,
he felt a shot,
but he fired back
toward the gunsmoke.
Very badly wounded, Patricia fell dying into his arms.

Before dying she told him,
"I did it because I love you.
I knew you were seeing another woman,
and the jealousy was too great to bear.
I would rather see you dead
than see you in another woman's arms."
(Performed by Los Tigres del Norte)

Perhaps one of the most classic narcocorrido tales of betrayal (and tragedy) can be found in an early and very popular narcocorrido, "Contrabando y Traición." In this somewhat unusual story, a woman (Camelia) is participating in a drug deal and shipment with a man, Emilio, who is presumed to be her lover or partner. But when the deal is done, he tells her he is off to San Francisco to the one he loves. The spurned lover, Camelia, shoots him and disappears with all the money. In this well-known story, it could be said that the romantic ballad roots of the corrido have blended with the narcocorrido, placing the story, along with its narcotrafficking context, in the body of regularized situations in which romantic tragedy can occur.

Contrabando y Traición
They departed from San Isidro on their way to Tijuana.
The tires of the car were full of marijuana.
They were Emilio Varela and Camelia, the Texan.

Passing through San Clemente, immigration stopped them.
They asked for their papers and asked them where they were
    from.
She was from San Antonio, a woman of heart.

If a woman loves a man, she will give her life for him,
but you need to be careful if she feels hurt.
Betrayal and contraband don't go together.

When they arrived in Los Angeles, they went on to Hollywood.
In a dark alley they changed the four tires.
That's where they left the weed and that's where they were paid.

Emilio said to Camelia, "Today I tell you good-bye.
With your share of the money, you can start a new life.
I'm going to San Francisco with the one who owns my heart."

Seven gunshots were heard, as Camelia killed Emilio.
A gun thrown on the ground was all the police found.

No one heard anything again, about the money or about
   Camelia.
(Performed by Los Tigres del Norte)

The next example is "Mis Tres Animales" (My Three Animals), by
Los Tucanes de Tijuana. This is a very well known narcocorrido
that combines elements of humor, wordplay, and boasting about
the lifestyle of the narcotrafficker. In this sense, it is not at all
like the classic corrido tale of a tragic event. It does, however, contain the ubiquitous reference to inevitable death and is closed with
a warning of sorts, not to the police or authorities, but to potential
drug users: "If you can't bullfight, then stay out of the ring."[3] It also
contains some key elements of the narcotrafficker's appeal: the element of social mobility from poverty to wealth, and not-so-subtle
jibes at the predominance of American products (the reference to
selling more than McDonald's).

Mis Tres Animales
I live off three animals
that I love as my life.
With them I make money,
and I don't even buy them food.
They are stupid animals,
my parakeet [cocaine], my rooster [marijuana], and my goat
   [heroin].

In California and Nevada,
in Texas and Arizona,
even out there in Chicago,
I have some people
who sell my animals
more than hamburgers
sold at McDonald's.

I learned to live life
until I had money.
I don't deny that I was poor
and that I was a mule skinner.
Now I am a great gentleman.
The gringos covet my pets.

Death is always near me,
but I don't know how to give in.
I know the government hunts me,

even under the sea,
but there's a way around everything,
and my hiding place hasn't been found.

Too much money
is also very dangerous.
That's why I spend it
with my good friends.
And when the women see it,
their eyes pop out.

They say that my animals
are going to finish the people off.
But it's not required
to place it in front of them.
My animals are brave.
If you can't bullfight, then stay out of the ring.

In a similar vein, though blunter and not quite as clever as "Animales," is "Me Gusta Ponerle al Polvo" (I Like to Do Cocaine), a boastful yet fatalistic description of the narrator's life as a trafficker and a user. (It may reference an actual trafficker.) While this corrido celebrates some high-profile elements of "the life," including the element of risk, it is also a dark testament to an existence as a marked man, a target, and the inevitable closeness to death ("I walk behind death because of the way I live"). Of the narcocorridos presented thus far, this is the only one with a farewell, or despedida, in anything like the classic manner.

Me Gusta Ponerle al Polvo

I like risky action, I like to do cocaine.
I know many hunt me, and for many I am in the way.

I walk right behind death because of the way I live.
I like taking risks, I like to do cocaine.
I know many hunt me, and for many I am in the way.

There are many following in my footsteps, so going out is not
    as fun.
Many places I go and many stare me down.
I know I'd make a good trophy for many of my enemies.

On the ranch El Zapatío, I have a beautiful blonde.
I'm going to see her soon, I like her because she is affectionate.
She's pretty and vain and I'm gonna make her my wife.

For all of those who hunt me, I'm gonna give you a piece of
   advice:
Pleasure is felt on the inside, and I want to remind you,
I like to enjoy life to the fullest, and money is made for
   spending.

With these lines I say farewell, I like always to be fair.
Any young woman who isn't mine, I'll take her from her mate.
I'm a friend of all men and to none will I back down.
(Performed by Exterminador)

The two narcocorridos that follow come from a compilation
produced and distributed by a recording studio that, as described
later in this chapter, is known for its "raw" portrayals of the
narcotrafficker persona. The persona characterized in these corridos is clearly reduced to its swaggering, boasting, risk-taking,
women-chasing, death-defying, fighting-cock minimum (regarding
the latter, the second of these corridos is called *The Rooster Player*).
These are street caricatures, but important nonetheless, because
they are part of a popular image as portrayed to one degree or another in the current media-hyped market for narcocorridos. As you
will notice, there is no reference here to social themes typical of
corridos, though (as discussed in Chapter 4) the assertion of a narcotrafficker identity via a medium independent of state discourse has
been considered, in itself, a social statement (Astorga 1997). In each
there are coded references to weapons—the "goat's horn" (AK-47
with a curved clip) or "special 38." In "El Toro Bravo" (The Angry
Bull) there is clear reference to a specific gang: the RV. Both these
corridos may reference actual individuals.

El Toro Bravo
Make way for me, Gentlemen,
I am here to sing
a corrido in honor of an angry bull
because he's a loyal friend
He's from the "Los Cortijos" ranch,
very close to Coleocal.

Even though he's a calm man,
I'll give you some advice.
Don't get in his way
if you want to make it to old age.
When you provoke a bull
death is not too far.

Gentlemen, the angry bull
always carries in his belt
a super 38,
handles decorated with gold.
Every time it's been offered [a chance]
it's never stayed quiet.

Don't close those paths
because around there goes a man.
No one knows what he carries.
Why know what he hides?
And many, for knowing it,
have died and never responded.

(Arriba Sinaloa, Capamavel. The RV!)

To brighten the stars,
to heat the sun,
to spend money,
to win recognition
for honest friendships,
the angry bull, Sir.

He's never short of money;
he does everything well.
He has intelligence to spare;
he accomplishes his duties
When things are done right,
you live better than a king.

How rough the water is
when you can't even see one shrimp?
Manuel is the angry bull,
a man with much power.
Good-bye men from the mountains,
Greetings from RV.
(Performed by Los Truenos de Sinaloa)[4]

El Gallo Jugado (The Rooster Player)
They're saying around there
that I'm going to get shot
because I'm fond of women
and for prohibited business.
I know many who want to
cut off my path.

If I bring green bills,
it's because I walk in danger.
I'm not afraid of bullets.
I carry a goat's horn [AK-47].
And those who don't want to believe it,
jump to the spray [of my bullets].

If it's about women,
I like to bet my luck.
I'm not afraid of bullets,
I have what I need to defend myself.
Death must be pretty
if they kill me face to face.

I like to take the band
Sinaloa style.
Give me pure corridos
and let the drums play.
I'm one of the rooster players
where the poppy grows.

Those who are in the business
should never trust anyone,
because even your best friend
can betray you,
and either he'll be sent to the cemetery
or you'll end up in prison.

For those who want to kill me,
I want to give you some advice:
It's better that you don't look for me,
because you'll find me.
And my goat's horn?
I'll make it bray.

This job is nice and
I'm not thinking of leaving it,
because I have plenty of women
and money to spend.
But this is dangerous business,
if anyone is thinking of joining in.
(Performed by Los Cuacos del Norte)

Then there are the narcocorridos that are about specific and well-known traffickers or druglords, such as Caro Quintero, Amado Carillo Fuentes, or Pablo Acosta. The following example is a story about Pablo Acosta, drug lord in the 1980s in the area of Ojinaga, south of Juárez near the Texas border. Again, there are familiar themes: the implication that he was a victim of treachery; his bravery and skill against even "the Devil" (Vecías, presumably a Mexican law enforcement official); and his tragic end, where his brother and men are killed with him.

El Zorro de Ojinaga (The Fox of Ojinaga)
He watched the border under Uncle Sam's orders.
He hunted down terrorists, those who knew how to kill,
the Fox of Ojinaga, Pablo Acosta Villareal.

But it was said that other orders were given.
They said he brought down planes with cocaine to start,
but now that he is dead, no one can contradict him.

Confidence and dominance are the weakness of the valiant.
Don't trust compliments, not even from family.
Even the most astute of foxes are trapped among their own
    people.

From the skies in Arizona, they tried to bring him down.
They sent Vecías, it was said, with a Mirage motor,
but the Fox with his Cessnas made the Devil look bad.

They killed his brother, who was his right-hand man,
and later at the ranch they charged the rent [killed more of his
    men].
But because he's dead now, it's not like they can contradict
    him.
(Performed by Los Tigres del Norte)

In this small sample, narcocorridos, at least lyrically, may be seen to share a number of characteristics of classic or traditional corridos, if not so much in form, then in the "editorial storytelling," boasting, antagonistic orientation toward the (unnamed) authorities or the United States, and, in some cases, a sense of (inevitable) tragedy. Like classic corridos, these corridos include the charismatic and heroic protagonist with which the Mexican audience identifies, a worldview dominated by "antagonistic, often Anglo-American forces" with whom the hero must contend (Saldívar 1986, p. 12), and an oral narrative.

As noted, the subject matter and nature of the conflict is, of course, somewhat different in classic corridos and narcocorridos, though there are more similarities between narcocorridos and the tequilero corridos of the Prohibition era. While there are ample references to conflicts with the authorities, both Mexican and American, there are also numerous references to treachery and the general danger of "the life." Many of the references to treachery are about narcotraffickers who are sold out or exposed by informers — sometimes girlfriends. There is a clear sense that few people can be trusted. Finally, the narcotrafficker character typically does not have the kind of "people's hero" image that classic corrido heroes often had (where, in addition to their heroic deed, they were said to be brave and true, loved their mother, etc.). Yet this is a fine distinction, because they are presented in many cases as antagonists of a corrupt and hypocritical authority structure, whether Mexican or American. Moreover, corridos tell specific stories, and whether or not the characters or action portrayed in the stories are "heroic" is a determination made, in large part, by the way in which characters of the type portrayed resonate with images and situations that, in themselves (apart from a specific characterization in the narrative) have heroic elements for the community of listeners. That is something which will be brought out further in the interview and observation data discussed below.

Coded Terms and Phrases Used in Narcocorridos

As noted, narcocorridos, in contrast to traditional corridos, utilize a specialized argot, a "narcojargon." Some terms or phrases found in narcocorridos include the following:

Cuerno de chivo—literally, "goat's horn," but commonly used to refer to an AK-47 assault rifle, weapon of choice in the narcoworld and a virtual folk item. This term, more than many of the others in the specialized argot, was common knowledge among almost everyone I talked with during this research. (The reference to "horn" probably comes from the AK-47's prominent curved bullet clip.)

"El rey del cielo"—lord of the skies; refers to Amado Carillo Fuentes, infamous head of the Juárez cartel until his mysterious death in 1997. The reference is derived from the fleet of airplanes he used to transport drugs across the border with the United States.

Burros or *mulas*—carriers of drugs across the border; usually a mid- or lower-level person in the operation at large.

Animales—drugs or drug habits with which an animal name is correlated, e.g., *gallo*, or rooster, a joint.

Bola de chicle—literally, "gumball"; heroin. May also refer to a
law enforcement net, which is "sticky."
Hierba verde, hierba buena, hierba mala—marijuana.
Perico (parakeet), *chiva* (female kid), *carga blanca* (white load),
cola sin cola (literally, "tail without a tail"), *polvo* (powder),
la buena, la fina—all often used for cocaine.

And note the following phrases, which clearly play on rural or agricultural usages and images:[5]

"Que bonita se ven mis vacas con colitas de borrego"—a phrase
that would commonly be used to describe cows: "How nice
my cows look with tails like lambs." But if the word *pacas* is
used instead of *vacas*, the sentence means "How nice my
packed [or packets of] marijuana looks."
"Aprendí a hacer las cuentas contando los costales"—a phrase
that, in a normal farming context, would roughly mean "I
learned [from a young age] how to count the bushels of food."
In a narcocontext, it means "I learned [from a young age] how
to count the bushels of marijuana."
"Ganado sin garrapata"—a phrase that, in a farming context,
refers to "cattle with no ticks." In a narco context, it means
"the finest marijuana available, with no seeds."

Notice how several of these coded phrases (or versions of them) are
used in "Pacas de a Kilo" (Kilo Sacks), a well-known narcocorrido
(included here in both Spanish and English):

Pacas de a Kilo (Kilo Sacks)
Me gusta andar por la sierra, me crié entre los matorrales.
Allí aprendí a hacer las cuentas, nomás contando costales.
Me gusta burlar las redes, que tienden los federales.

[I like being up in the mountains, I grew up in the thicket.
That's where I learned the finances, by counting the sacks.
I love escaping the traps set by the federal police.]

Muy pegadito a la sierra, tengo un rancho ganadero,
ganados sin garrapatas, que llevo pal extranjero.
Que chulas se ven mis vacas, con colitas de borrego.

[Right next to the mountains, I have a cattle ranch,
(where I keep my) cattle without ticks, which I take to the
foreign land.
My cows look so good with their lamb tails.]

El Tigre a mi me acompaña, porque ha sido un gran amigo,
maestro en la pista chica, además muy precavido.
Él sabe que en esta chamba, no es bueno volar dormido.

[The Tiger accompanies me because he has been a true friend,
He is a master of the short runway, he's also very cautious
He knows that in this business, it's no good to sleep when you
    fly.]

Por el negocio que tengo, por donde quiera me paseo.
no me gusta que presumen, tampoco me miren feo.
Me gusta que me platiquen, pero no todo les creo.

[With the type of business I have, wherever I travel,
I don't like those who boast or those who give me nasty looks.
I like conversation, but don't believe everything I hear.]

Por ahí andan platicando, que un día me van a matar.
No me asustan las culebras, yo sé perder y ganar.
Ahí traigo un cuerno de chivo, para él que le quiera entrar.

[There's talk that one day I'm gonna get killed.
I'm not afraid of snakes, I know how to lose or win.
I've got an AK-47 for whoever wants to give it a try.]

Adiós tierra de Coahuila, de Sinaloa y Durango,
De Sonora y Tamaulipas, Chihuahua te andas quedando.
Si me quieren conocer, en Juárez me ando paseando.

[Farewell, Coahuila, Sinaloa, and Durango,
Sonora and Tamaulipas. Chihuahua, you're staying behind.
If they want to meet me, I'll be traveling through Juárez.]
(Performed by Los Tigres del Norte)

In addition to the liberal use of rural metaphor or code, this particular narcocorrido truly encapsulates many of the themes discussed thus far, including personal bravado; the ability to handle
risk; closeness to and intimate knowledge of the land; affection
for the region; the attraction or "game" of evading the authorities;
the construction of drug trafficking as a worthy business for which
knowledge, skill, and personal efficacy are required; and the inevitability of death (together with the willingness to challenge it). As
a corrido, "Pacas" also includes a classic-style despedida.

The Listening Audience: The "Narcocorrido Community"

A key for understanding listener (and, for that matter, producer) interpretation of narcocorridos lies in what McDowell (1981, p. 45) has called the "ballad community"—speaking of corridos as ballads—a "hypothesized human community which supports an active ballad tradition while providing the cosmological orientation represented in those ballads." The community to which he refers is the larger set of people who listen to narcocorridos. Here I will add *actively* listen, because in their current mass-marketed form, corridos are played on the radio to many who may hear them, but who may not pay any more attention to them than they would to other things on the radio. This set of people (the active listeners) is the audience that, to some degree or another, is familiar with the referential base from which the narcocorridos draw.

Who listens to narcocorridos? This was, of course, a key initial question set out in my research plan, and was the first question typically asked in interviews (see the interview guides in Appendix 1). Identifying the listening population (or who people say is the listening population) is an important indicator with respect to social stratification, because it says much about whom the narcocorrido themes appeal to, the social referents of the message.

This could not have been clearer than in one interview conducted with an executive at a company that manages a number of radio stations based in the Juárez area (but heard in El Paso as well). The executive specifically broke out the listening audience of all six or so of his company's stations into four socioeconomic classes, from A (upper) to D (lower). He characterized the station that played mostly pop romantic ballads as appealing to groups A and B; the news station, to groups A, B, and C. Another station playing a pop mix was said to appeal most to groups C and D, including a large segment of working-class listeners who are the bulk of the workforce in the maquilas. Significantly, the radio station that has a long tradition of playing norteño music, including corridos and (now) narcocorridos, was clearly classified as targeting group D, said to be lower class and including many who were transplants to Juárez from rural areas. This station broadcasts on AM only.

Disk jockeys and radio personnel at the last radio station, which I will call "La Banda," noted that they played a mix of norteño music that included romantic corridos, older corridos, *cumbias* and *banda* music, and some narcocorridos. They acknowledged the popularity of narcocorridos, but said that they were not really "radio." They claimed that narcocorridos were more a music of the street, an *underground* music, because they were *fuerte* (strong, controversial). And so they are. Walk along Avenida Juárez when the traffic is heavy, or come to a stoplight in many border towns, and you may hear narcocorridos blasting from the radio of a truck next to you. Walk into any *discotería* in Juárez, and you will find rows of narcocorrido CDs and tapes. This pattern is even truer since many radio stations (at least in Mexico) have informally agreed to stop or at least reduce their airing of narcocorridos. Yet according to one radio disk jockey, "In every house there is a narcocorrido tape."

And, without a doubt, a part of the listening audience includes those involved in drug trafficking. Why? Because the narcocorrido is part of *el mundo, la vida* (the world, the life) of the drug trade. Narcocorridos, along with other norteño music (and even mariachi music), form part of the backdrop to the narcotrafficker identity. A common scenario: When a narcotrafficker is throwing a party, or there is a funeral or a wedding, a norteño band will be hired to play. The celebration may last for days at, for example, the trafficker's ranch or big house, and the band will be brought in for the duration.

Still, describing the totality of the listening audience is not that simple. When Los Tucanes perform in El Paso or Juárez, the stadium or concert venue is likely to be packed, with the "usual" listening audience of lower- and working-class individuals, but also college or high school students. Based on my observations and interviews, it is fair to say that the Mexican American adults who listen, however, tend to be those who do not regularly engage in or subscribe to Anglo cultural practices, beliefs, and symbols (I am using this description as a more accurate substitute for calling these listeners "less acculturated"). They may be recent migrants or individuals whose family and important social ties are on both sides of the border. This group listens primarily to Mexican and Latino music. At the same time, my valued friends Jorge and his fiancée, Carlota (pseudonyms), do not come from elite families; quite the opposite. Yet they are both well educated and politically involved and do not themselves generally listen to narcocorridos, though they are very familiar with them as well as with the world in which they are well received. They, however, grew up and live in Juárez; they are not migrants and do not come from a rural background.

For adult audiences in the research site, corridos (including narcocorridos) are heard as recorded music in the car, in bars (often after work), on jukeboxes, via live corrido/norteño bands in clubs or cantinas, or at home:

In cantinas and bars, performances may take many forms. In one of the tiny, working class cantinas in the narrow streets of the old Juárez mercado, I sat at the bar, drinking from a bottle pulled from the ice chest on the cement floor near the end of the bar. By the door, a squat, thick-bodied woman with a very short red dress and heels leaned against the wall, eyeing the meager collection of customers with a kind of tired displeasure. In the opposite corner, an impromptu norteño trio was setting up—a standup bass, accordion, and guitar. They began to play a collection of norteño tunes, including corridos. Impromptu performances like this are not unusual. In other cantinas I was in, I also saw single musicians who came in with a guitar, playing a wide range of ballads, corridos (including narcocorridos) and other norteño music for a small fee.

One interview respondent, a young man in his late teens or early twenties, said that his father listened to corridos all the time with his friends, that they reminded his father of his home state in Mexico, because they are often sung by and about people from Michoacán, Chihuahua, Sonora, Durango, and Sinaloa—states north of Mexico City with significant rural populations and from which many immigrants come (and which are major drug-growing and -producing areas). This is significant, because, according to interviews with recording industry respondents, there is a large and growing market for narcocorridos and norteño music in general among the Hispanic/Latino immigrant community in areas such as Los Angeles, Chicago, Florida, the San Joaquin and Central Valley areas of California, in cities in the Midwest, some parts of the Pacific Northwest, and all along the U.S.-Mexico border (as well as in Mexico at large).

On the radio in the Juárez/El Paso area, there is a station, as mentioned earlier, which features norteño music, including corridos. This station has been a fixture in the area for some seventy years. I had the benefit of being able to talk with several station staff members, including disk jockeys, who said that they play narcocorridos, but in a mix with other norteño music. Young people, they said, are the primary requestors of narcocorridos. In the studios of La Banda (the radio station), I watched as one disk jockey handled an entire show specializing in corridos. The equipment was old, and he answered all telephone calls himself while operating the equipment and chattering in a steady stream of often-humorous dialog. The range of call-ins to the station was varied, with many callers talking at length, sometimes about family or local situations. The atmosphere on the show was decidedly informal, and almost like an extended family of sorts; other station staff members who happened to be in the studio sometimes joined in a conversation. Yet the station played narcocorridos on this program, and there was a sense that these were just one of a piece with the other music being played, part of the general fabric.

I have also heard about radio programs devoted to narcocorridos: "La Hora de Chalino," exclusively devoted to the music of Chalino Sánchez; "Burros Norte," playing narcocorridos by a number of groups such as Los Huracanes; and a program that plays primarily Los Tucanes and other groups from Tijuana. According to one source, the latter two types of programs appear to be divided up on a semiterritorial basis: the "Burros" program plays mostly bands identified with the Juárez cartel; the other program focuses on bands associated with the Tijuana cartel and its flashier lifestyle.

Mexican and Mexican American youth who listen to narcocorridos (on both sides of the border), as noted, exist in a transcultural world, in which narcocorridos are consumed along with a melange of Anglo and world pop music. They recognize narcocorridos, to some extent, the same way they would gangsta rap—but gangsta rap that is more attuned to representations of daily reality and cultural idioms and themes that resonate with the Latino experience. I have drawn this conclusion from several sources: interview responses that refer to narcocorrido themes and descriptions (like those of gangsta rap) as reflective of daily life, of "how it is"; observations of youth (and others) at narcocorrido performances in which the performance is amplified by the audience, many of whom are dressed in styles associated with norteño music (and sometimes with narcotraffickers);[6] the way in which narcotraffickers are portrayed on the covers of some CDs and tapes (see photo section following page 130), which is in the style of gangsta rap, though with different clothing; and cultural/historical background material on corridos and their role. Even so, interview responses provide a clue to the complexity of the youth audience.

"Border youth," if such a term can be used to refer to adolescents and younger adults, were said in several interviews to group into the following categories. In the first category are *"cheros"* (note that this term was used in descriptions of youth and young adults, but it also refers to adults who dress or present themselves this way). Many who are narcotraffickers or affiliated in some way with the narcoworld are said to fall into this category, including older adolescents and young adults. The term "chero" (from the word "ran-

Plates 3a and b.
Youth project in
Colonia Bella Vista.

chero") refers to those who dress in the kind of clothing common to northern, rural Mexico and who are commonly seen where corridos and norteño music are played. I was interviewing three *"chavos,"* or youth, fifteen to eighteen years old, in a car parked in front of the small project run for youth by Jorge. We had gone there hoping to talk to a number of kids. The building was a small, beige storefront meeting hall in Colonia Bella Vista (Plates 3a and b), with paint faded and peeling, owned by a local baker's union. On that day it was closed for some reason, and the youth couldn't get in, so, as usual when this sort of thing happened, there was a lot of standing around, with Jorge conferring here and there. Finally, I just used the open car as a seat and sat and talked for a while to the three or four youth who were still there. One of them gave me a very elaborate description of chero style and talked about a kind of hierarchy among cheros, in part signaled by clothing and presentation: the large, wide belts with engraved or designed plate metal buckles, the boots (of lizard or alligator, if possible); the "cowboy-type" hat; *barbitos,* or frills, on shirts and jackets; and, as another of the youth said, nicknames.

Cheros sometimes put nicknames on their clothing, and, if they work in a maquila, may have the name of the maquila on their clothing somewhere, as if (said one respondent) they were a "jefe del mundo" (boss of the world). The domain of dress and power is itself an interesting phenomenon, and it comports with other interview comments about how one's place in the power hierarchy is evaluated via personal presentation: someone wearing too much "chero costumery" is viewed, derogatorily, as a *"superchero,"* someone who is trying too hard to impress, to create an image as a narcotrafficker with means, so to speak, or simply a person or employee with money. A superchero who is a drug dealer is typically perceived as low on the totem pole, someone who may have some money at this moment, but is just as likely to have none down the road. Narcotraffickers who are viewed as more powerful may dress in the chero style, but in a more restrained manner.

Related to this, some younger interview respondents seemed to affiliate images of individual power with "being in an organization." Organizations are headed by "el mero bueno" (the boss, or best one) and are composed of people who give orders as well as obey them.

At a small restaurant near one bar known to be a narcohangout, Jorge pointed out to me a man who looked to be in his mid-twenties, wearing a crisp yellow shirt, jeans, boots, a cowboy hat, and a wide belt—a restrained chero, so it seemed. He was preceded into the restaurant by two men who Jorge said were probably his bodyguards.

He followed them in and sat at a table to eat. No one in his entourage seemed to do anything until he did it first.

In the second category are *"cholos"*—primarily older youth, eighteen and above, who follow in dress and action the *pachuco* style (first popularized in the 1940s). This includes crisply pressed white shirts, very baggy khaki pants (preferably the Dickies brand), and hair nets. Cholos are neighborhood oriented; groups or gangs of cholos stick to their neighborhood, and their graffiti tends to focus on messages about their barrio. This graffiti is usually called *placazo.*

"Tumbados" are younger youth, approximately ages twelve to seventeen. Tumbados, who also call themselves *"cruwes"* (from "crews"?), listen to a combination of mostly American rock and hip-hop/rap music. Favorite rock bands include Motley Crüe and Marilyn Manson. Tumbados are said to wear baggies in the hip-hop style, but also baggy T-shirts with rock group names on them. They are not as neighborhood focused as cholos, and their graffiti tends to be more broadly social in orientation—messages against the police or the government, or about other social themes.

These descriptions make it clear that saying "youth" listen to narcocorridos is overly simplistic. There are groupings of youth, some who are more likely to listen to them than others.

And now there is also a substantial listening population outside of Mexico, in Central and Latin America, and among U.S. Latino populations not necessarily from Mexico.

Listener Interpretations

Much of the time, when asking people about corridos, I wanted to know how they were interpreted. For narcocorridos, I wanted to know how they were interpreted in general and, more specifically, how the narcotrafficker figure was viewed. A number of factors relevant to interpretation arose in these discussions.

Exclusivity versus Familiarity

As Paredes (1993, p. 84) and others have well noted, Mexican verbal art is performance and, as such, is filled with nuanced and idiomatic usages, humor, use of indirect language, euphemism, double and triple meaning, allusive language, circumlocution, and other forms of wordplay. What we see may or may not be what we get, in a direct sense. Or, it is one of several things that we get. Narcocorridos, more so than classic corridos, take from this tradition. The code words and phrases described earlier are an example of this.

There is an element of *exclusivity* that pertains to the narco-corrido listening community. In contrast to traditional corridos, many narcocorridos are full of code words, or "narcojargon," which are usually double-entendre references to actors or objects within the narcoworld. The presence of code words may imply that (1) a significant proportion of the listening audience is either involved in the drug trade or otherwise knows the code words because they exist in close proximity to the drug trade; (2) narcojargon itself has a kind of "chic" appeal, where understanding it means that one has a "dangerous side" or something similar. To see this marked in conversation, simply ask someone the meaning of a particular narco code word or phrase. If they know it, the explanation is likely to be accompanied by a slight smile or other gesture that indicates that they know the special status of such words as signifiers of activity that is dangerous and unsanctioned. I would argue that this element of exclusivity in narcocorridos is not part of the ethos of classic corridos.

However, there is another way to interpret listener understanding of these code words. Many of the terms may actually be familiar enough to the listening audience that the issue of exclusivity is understood as a parody, or as irony. In this interpretation, the code words, while familiar, are presented as if exclusive, making a sort of sport out of the pretense of exclusivity, and possibly even carrying the message: "If you think these words are exclusive or cryptic, then you are truly not 'with it.'"

Music and Sound

A second key to interpretation consistent with all listener interviews is that, for corridos, the music itself is important in framing the message of the songs, even while the lyrics are the essence of the performance. It could be said that the music is basically similar for most corridos, and that the musical sound intersects with other related norteño (northern Mexico, border area) music styles, such as the banda. As noted earlier, the performance of these corridos includes rhyme and rhythmic elements that give them a kind of "bounce" and danceability. This kind of music is played at settings marked as festive and in other collective settings. At the same time, the sound of the music itself adds an important ambience that frames the genre as *country*, from rural areas. Thus the sound, in itself, does create a link between the music and the home regions of so many residents—temporary or permanent—of Juárez and El Paso. In interviews, some respondents did say that they listened to it because it was a reminder of home, a reminder of a rural identity. And, at a number of performances I attended, including one large performance in El Paso by the famous (narco)corrido group Los Tigres del Norte, the audience was highly enthusiastic, sometimes responding with a kind of yelping shout or cheer—the *grito*. While there were many seated in the chairs and stands at this show, the center floor was largely reserved for dancing. The band played on a large stage with a backdrop that was a large mural of green hills, palm trees, and small white villages—terrain typical of Sinaloa and neighboring states in northwestern Mexico.

Lyrics and Narrative

At the same time, the lyrics are the enduring essence of the performance, as would be expected, given the historical role of corridos. (Most of the time, when people talk about corridos they talk about what the corridos *say*.) As such, corridos are a narrative form as much as or more than a musical form, which comports with their traditional role. This is the case whether the lyrics are viewed as serious, as real, as ironic, or as humorous. In all these cases, they still *carry the impact*. People still say that such-and-such a corrido is *about something*.

Performer and Celebrity

That being said, narcocorridos, as a modern media version of the classic corrido, now also rely on the image of the performer as a key element of meaning, and so take their place within the larger industry of media production. Narcocorrido bands have become "stars," and there is even an accompanying, and intertwined, genre of narcotrafficker film (not investigated in this research). The performer thus has a social role which in itself channels interpretation. Performers are, as I discuss later in this book, "celebretized." I view this as a departure from the way in which traditional corridos presented their message—where the singer was more of a medium or interpreter (albeit a creative interpreter), carrying the story from one place to another, and where the story was a socially constructed narrative of how things are, passed from community to community.

Performance Atmosphere

Finally, there is something about narcocorridos that draws attention and carries a certain energy during a performance, more so than for corridos that are not about narcotraffickers. Again, at the Los Tigres show I attended, when the Tigres sang narcocorridos, there was a noticeable crowd response, a swell of noise and applause, though in this context it was largely framed as festive, yet somehow vicarious as well, in the manner of professional wrestling or even cartoons. Exaggerated gunshot sounds and lights went off on stage, and when that happened, most of the audience treated it as great fun, part of the carnival atmosphere of the moment. People shouted; men lifted their girlfriends. At norteño bars where I saw live music played, there was often an analogous energy, and I believe it is generally typical of such shows. For example, one review of a Los Tucanes show in a largely migrant community near Monterey, California, describes the atmosphere as follows (Collier 1997):

> [T]he 2,000 fans in attendance went wild when the band ripped into its new hit, "La Piñata." The song tells of a druglord's party with a piñata full of bags of cocaine. . . . As he [Mario Quintero, Los Tucanes' lead singer] sang, a stream of young women jumped up on stage from the audience to kiss him and the other three band members. In fact, it seemed as if the entire female audience did the same thing during the hour-and-40 minute concert. Young mothers dragging their babies handed them off to friends, jumped up, planted their red-lipstick kisses on sweaty cheeks one by one and jumped down.

This issue of energy or power came up in a number of interviews, and indeed I have seen it: when a narcocorrido is played, the crowd is energized. A radio DJ explained that "they [corridos] give a special feeling, a Mexican feeling." Corridos and narcocorridos are also the songs one plays later in the party, after drinking alcohol, when the feelings are more intense, he said.

Building on these factors, narcocorridos are interpreted in a wide range of ways that depend on who the listener is and in what context he or she is listening. The multiplicity of interpretations include the following.

Interpreting Narcocorridos as Reality

Corridos, while not strict recountings of facts or events, are typically grounded in real events and contexts that are understood by the listening community. Narcocorridos, according to data collected for this study, follow this pattern and are interpreted as a reflection of reality by many (though not all) of the listening community.

Interviews with adults, or interviews in which adults were discussed, indicated that adults (that is, persons older than age twenty-five or so) from rural areas in northern Mexico, particularly in the sierra, listen to the stories told in the narcocorridos as a reflection of several realities. One is the degree to which the drug trade, and the growing of drug-related plants (opium poppies, marijuana), has been for a long time closely integrated into the life of many rural villages. For example, one respondent in El Paso, a man in his sixties, recalled that, even in the late 1940s, in his small village in Sinaloa, there was a man who grew opium poppies between the rows of maize. The man would pay him and his friends a peso (a lot of money for them at the time) to take a razor blade and slice all the poppy bulbs so that the "milk" would run. Apparently, the milk granulates after a day or two, and the man would later come by and collect the granulated poppy milk. Another respondent told of how, in traveling through small villages in northern Sonora, he saw that people often kept plastic bags of cocaine or marijuana in their houses as a resource to sell whenever necessary. Most people, he said, were well aware that the drug trade was illegal or otherwise disfavored, but it was so much a part of daily life that people remained involved. At the same time, it was a cutthroat and competitive business, and people kept guns around and were not hesitant to use them if necessary. Three adult prisoners in the central Juárez jail (the *cereso*, short for *centro de readaptación social*, center for social readaptation) with whom I talked also spoke of the drug industry as a matter-of-fact, normal occurrence—a central part of the economy of their pueblos in southern Chihuahua, Michoacán, and Sinaloa. The narcotraffickers for them were "big men," providing wealth and jobs to the community.

Norteño musicians I know and talked with (I will call the group "Plata Norte") view narcocorridos, for the most part, as serious and, in many ways, like other corridos, as an integral part of the tapestry of community. Plata Norte was in fact tapped to write a corrido about a local trafficker group members knew and whom they viewed as a "humble man, with a good heart, loved by the community," despite his involvement in trafficking. His life, and his death, were significant in the community, period. What is even more revealing is that the community-related meaning these songs have for Plata Norte's members can exist simultaneously with other sentiments that would, on the surface, appear contradictory. I, in fact,

Plate 4. Colonia adjacent to the youth project in Colonia Alta Vista.

came to know the group through a key member who helped run a local substance abuse/violence prevention program.

Youth interviewed on both the U.S. and the Mexican sides who live in barrios or other areas (e.g., colonias) where there is a high prevalence of drug trade activity, gangs, and the like, view narcocorridos, on the one hand, as a reflection of how it is on the streets. This characterization is virtually identical to oft-heard comments about the "reality" described in gangsta rap. Narcocorridos are viewed as telling it how it is not just because of the exact circumstances of the narratives—which often refer to the drug trade in and from Mexico (as opposed to action on the streets of U.S. cities themselves)—but also because of the attitudes, character types, and environment of risk that it presents. For these listeners, narcocorridos thus reflect an "atmospheric of the street." The music is even called "hard-core," according to a narcocorrido performer and producer interviewed during extended fieldwork in Los Angeles. However, there is in these responses a Marcus-like problem of not knowing exactly where to locate the source of these representations. Do they really come "from the streets"? Or are they a mixture of what youth see on the streets and in other media representations (television, narcocorridos) about these same streets. My sense is that it is weighted toward the latter, because, as will be explained more fully below, the narcotrafficker image is co-created by the mass media and day-to-day practice.

Not that the streets aren't hard enough. In many parts of Juárez,

Plate 5. Youth project being developed in Colonia Alta Vista.

the poverty is bleak. The drug trade, and those involved in it, are a big part of the picture. There are addicts younger than ten years old on the streets, addicted to drugs dumped on the Mexican side that didn't make it across for one reason or another. Some two hundred young women (many of them maquila workers) have been murdered in the past couple of years in Juárez. There is a gang issue in many border towns. In Juárez, I occasionally conducted interviews with youth at a fledgling youth project in Colonia Alta Vista (Plates 4 and 5). To get there, I would drive with Jorge along a road heading west near the border, turn up into a hilly area through a series of dirt roads, then finally turn up one rutted road to the top of a hill. On the top of that hill, a flat spot and, at one corner, a forlorn cinder block shed covered in graffiti. It was tiny, maybe fifteen feet by twenty feet. Walk past it, look over the edge of the hill, and there was a dirt soccer field below, with cracking cement bleachers running up the side of the hill to the top. Behind the shed on the other side was a gully, filled with trash. Jorge's friend was helping rebuild the shed into a youth center and had planted a few trees around the perimeter. Between Jorge and his friend, *abrazos* (hugs) always—two human beings in the service of others. Truly. Jorge's friend was also working on wiring the inside of the shed so that he could put in some lights. At one side, a Ping-Pong table. Four kids, probably about eight to twelve years old, were playing. Several other kids were sitting by the door, and Jorge, who knew them all, greeted them, made jokes. Sometimes when I was there, a few other kids would wander down the dirt road that came from the rows of tiny colonia houses on the hill. One evening, it was getting late and I was up there with Jorge's fiancée, Carlota, who had given me a ride and was trying to find Jorge. A dusty police car pulled up, possibly thinking that we were up to something. Carlota waved them off.

In several other interviews, there is support for the view that narcocorridos reflect a mass-mediated understanding of the street as much as an immediate understanding. One respondent in El Paso, whose circle of friends included several involved in trafficking, said that the explicit narco-lyrics of bands like the recently popular Los Tucanes de Tijuana were viewed by these friends as cheap marketing, as the talk of "wannabees" who didn't know the reality of the narcoworld. These kinds of lyrics were contrasted with the narcocorridos of Los Tigres del Norte, whose lyrics include a broader range of sentiments and utilize much more subtle and coded ways of talking about trafficking, with less of the glib, glamorized, and oversimplistic portrayals of bravado, money, and women. The subtlety and depth was viewed by this respondent as an indication that they (Los Tigres) were much more aware of the daily business, and the ups and downs, of the drug trade.

Moreover, there is at least one website devoted to narcocorridos (http://www.atomico.com.ar/info/narcocorridos.htm, based in Argentina), and this site, in reviewing the most recent CD by Los Tigres del Norte, reported listener reaction to narcocorridos (as with corridos in general) as including the following representative comments, typical of the "reflection of reality" pattern described above:

> "A mí me gustan los corridos porque son los hechos reales de nuestro pueblo" (I like corridos because they are the things that are really happening with our people), and "Sí, a mí también me gustan porque en ellos se canta la pura verdad" (Yes, I like corridos, too, because in them they sing the pure truth).

Again, these comments are almost exactly the same as listener comments reported in show reviews. Reviewing a Los Tucanes show, young audience members were quoted as saying, "I like Los Tucanes because they sing about what's really happening"; "Drug trafficking is part of life, so why ignore it? And it's not all bad, anyway. It creates prosperity" (Collier 1997).

There is another aspect of narcocorridos-as-reality which I found fascinating and even surprising, given the current mass-media hype surrounding the genre. The Arizona-based norteño band Plata Norte explained to me that, at almost every one of their shows (they perform all along the border and in Mexico and the United States), someone will come from the audience and give them handwritten lyrics, or a home-recorded tape, for a corrido about something that happened in their town or area. These offerings are requests that the band make a corrido out of the material. The events recounted in the lyrics may be a local tragedy (e.g., a woman whose sister was killed came to the band and asked them to do a corrido about her sister), or, in some cases, a drug trafficking situation, the latter because such situations are everyday facts of life in some border areas and northern Mexican communities.

In any case, even some of the larger and more famous norteño groups (e.g., Los Tigres) will take such requests and make some of them into corridos that they perform in shows. This "bottom-up" transfer, by an interesting twist, thus retains a key element of the community base of corridos, which is an important means of reflecting reality akin to that originally found in what I have called classic corridos.

Interpreting Corridos as Political Statements

Political undertones and overtones are present in a number of the corridos I reviewed, but, as noted below, these elements are not necessarily inherent in the character of the narcotrafficker himself (most narcotraffickers, at this time, are male), which differs from the political aspect of traditional corridos, where it is the hero and subject of the corrido who either makes the political statement or whose actions constitute a political statement. Oftentimes, where political content exists in a narcocorrido I reviewed, it is a statement by the corridistas. For example, note the following stanzas from "El General," quoted earlier:

Different countries are certified by the Americans.
They don't want drugs to exist.
They say drugs are dangerous.
But tell me, who certifies
the United States?

Mexico has tried honestly and hard
to apprehend the narcotraffickers.
The Americans buy the cocaine.
They'll pay any price for it.
They say they don't want drugs to exist,

but [when it comes to certification] they give themselves a big
    break.

This is presented as an aside in the song. It is not in itself part of
the story being related, but an add-on.

During preliminary fieldwork in El Paso/Juárez during July 1998,
I was told that a trafficker had openly been building some sort of
bridge over the Rio Grande between Juárez and El Paso—which at
that point was just a large cement channel—presumably over which
he intended to transport drugs. Now if this is true, why would he do
such a thing in the open? There is no chance that the bridge would
be completed, because the U.S. Border Patrol and Mexican police
were right there and it was bound to be destroyed. The only conclusion that I could draw is that it was simply a statement, a physical
and visible equivalent of saying, "I am someone. I do what I want.
You . . . all of you . . . do not have power over me. I do not cringe or
bow before you."

This sentiment is clearly, even starkly, expressed in many of the
narcocorrido lyrics, to wit:

Consulado Privado (Private Consulate)
Los gringos tienen poder
pero no para nosotros
Los pollos que les pasamos
no piensen que muy pocos
Aunque han puesto mil barreras
nos han pelado los ojos.

The gringos have power,
but not over us.
The undocumenteds we send them
are not just a few, let me tell you.
Though they have put up a thousand obstacles,
their eyes are still closed to us.
(Performed by Los Tucanes de Tijuana)

For some interviewees, the source of their admiration for the narcotraffickers sung about in narcocorridos had to do specifically with
narratives in which the narcotrafficker "defeated" or managed to
transport drugs past the police, Border Patrol, or other authorities.
Again, on the website, narcocorridos are described as "defeating"
the preference of "authorities" that these realities (the realities of
drugs and their related context) be "buried" by telenovelas and the

passage of time. Instead, the narcocorridos "impede forgetting, immortalize people and situations, and defeat the conventional interpretations about what is happening." These comments indicate that the traditional editorializing function of corridos is still understood to be part of narcocorridos. The position being taken here also falls into line with the historical antiauthoritarian content of many corridos. In this case, however, the authors of this website commentary are positioning narcocorridos in opposition to the stories told in other mass media, such as telenovelas. Interestingly, in other interviews, telenovelas are grouped with other media that are said to challenge tradition—at least with respect to gender roles and subjects long considered taboo for open discussion. There is even a corrido about George Bush the elder—a story about how he had a mafia that killed many people.

Interpreting Corridos as Heroic Tales or Allegories

The corrido as heroic tale or allegory is a key element in understanding the role and place of the narcotrafficker persona. First of all, as can be seen from the sample of lyrics themselves, there is a mixed message in the narcocorridos with respect to the glorification of drug trafficking (though I do not believe, as do Paredes and Herrera-Sobek, that this mixed message is solely a reflection of the moral ambivalence of the listening community as a whole with respect to the drug trade, because, as I note elsewhere, the role and position of traffickers varies by urban-rural dimensions, as counterposed against authority, and by other factors). The portrayal, as noted above, is one of power and daring, but also treachery, betrayal, and tragedy. Interestingly enough, in neither El Paso nor Juárez did I find many people who interpreted narcocorridos as tales of heroes in the manner of traditional corridos about, for example, Gregorio Cortez or Pancho Villa. This corresponds to the fact that, for the most part, respondents did not view traffickers themselves as heroes. In this sense, Paredes' and Herrera-Sobek's argument about the community sentiment reflected in narcocorridos is supported, though, as the discussion continues, I believe it will be evident that this is only part of the current "story."

Most respondents, even young ones, tended to view heroes of older corridos (e.g., Pancho Villa) as people who had a cause, who sacrificed for the community. The old corridos were about people who were assassinated, about people who had famous horses . . . and about land—about fighting for land, and for the people, said one young man. Few respondents thought narcotraffickers were heroes in this sense. Powerful and fearsome, yes. As "players" with money, women, and an aura of excitement, yes. As *valientes* (valiant, "men with balls"), or *vatos*, yes. As "big men," yes, in the sense that they were the ones (especially in rural areas south of Juárez) who often provided employment and various services to the community. Even—as noted above—as political foils or tricksters, confronting, undercutting, critiquing, and escaping both Mexican and American authorities. But not as "social heroes," at least in an overt sense. However, it is important to say that the distinction may be of only limited importance vis-à-vis research questions: if they are viewed as powerful and even as larger-than-life figures in all these senses, they are still *personas grandes* (big people), characters that occupy an ontological discourse removed at some level from the realm of the quotidian.

One of the first well-known modern narcotraffickers was Pedro Aviles Pérez, nicknamed "el Léon de la Sierra," or the Lion of the Sierra, after a guerrilla fighter in the hills of Michoacán. Most traffickers are well aware that it is in their interest to foster "legendary information" about themselves: Pablo Acosta, drug kingpin based in Ojinaga, Mexico, used to play up what became a "fabled" shootout with rival trafficker Fermín Arévalo that left him in sole control of a large territory. In fact, he had the shot-up Ford Bronco driven in the shootout placed on blocks at the highway entrance to Ojinaga, as a kind of monument to his legend (Poppa 1990).

Many youth on the U.S. side in El Paso also see the narcotraffickers whose exploits are documented in the corridos not as heroes, but as players, as people who have power, who are centers of action, danger, and thrills. This was true for both male and female respondents in our interviews. The narcotraffickers are just one kind of character who can be viewed as "crazy," as willing to take serious risks, so as to be the subject (said a former gang member and now gang prevention project director) of comments like "That fool did it!" (This sounds much like the oft-cited notion of "La Vida Loca"). Girls from a gang prevention program in El Paso clearly expressed a kind of delight in the bad or delinquent individual. Sometimes these girls dressed as cheros themselves and went to several clubs in El Paso that were known as narcotrafficker hangouts. They went to be near the action. And, indeed, the lyrics of many narcocorridos play up this image; "Mis Tres Animales" is a good example.

One day in El Paso, I interviewed several kids at a car wash near Carolina Avenue, south of I-10. The constant flow of I-10 hummed in the background. These were kids in Frank García's (pseudonym) gang prevention program. Frank himself had been in prison for some twenty years, and his arms were covered with tattoos. He was out now and ran a small program to work with kids who were involved in gangs or in other kinds of trouble. One youth, a short young man who appeared to be about sixteen or seventeen, was clearly a leader. He was a former gang member himself, but here he was acting as a sort of quality-assurance person for the car wash, checking the cars washed by other kids, resolving disputes. Frank talked to me about the attraction of the life, including the life portrayed in narcocorridos. "Kids," said Frank, "will do what they are validated for. You see a five-year-old girl putting a broom bristle in her arm as if a syringe. Her parents are probably injection users and laugh at her and say, 'Look what she's doing . . . she's *loca!*'" And the corridos sometimes make the trafficker role look easy. There is a hunger for glamour, for power. Again, according to Frank, "The father figure culturally is power. Where there is no father figure [around], they will seek power somehow."

I take the general reaction from respondents in Juárez, however, as incomplete, because viewing narcotraffickers as powerful players, but not as heroes, differs from what appeared to be more common in Los Angeles and from the views expressed by all respondents I contacted in the recording and music-marketing industry (see below) as well as some responses in Juárez/El Paso from people who came more recently from towns farther south of the border. Indeed, in a fairly recent interview (Rivera 1998), Los Tucanes' lead singer Mario Quintero said, "Hay muchos de ellos [narcotraffickers] que han ayudado al pueblo. Esa gente ayuda. Caro Quintero hizo escuelas, puso alumbrado en algunos pueblos. Hacía más que el gobierno. Ahí está también El Cochiloco, él fue verdadero benefactor. Entre ellos hay gente bien derecha." In effect, there are many narcotraffickers who are just and help the people, and who do more in this respect than the government.

As noted, the ambivalence of many respondents in El Paso/Juárez may be in part due to the nature of the drug trade in those cities. In Mexican states like Sinaloa, Michoacán, Durango, and Sonora, narcotraffickers are big men in the community, and the drug-production industry is an indigenous industry. At the border, in Juárez, the focus is on the "dirty end of the business": getting the drugs across the border, ensuring turf dominance for the Juárez cartel, punishing informers and others who threaten the trade, selling the drugs in Juárez that don't make it across the border, corruption of local officials, and the constant and fluid display of power and wealth in ways large and small that is part of the business of establishing and maintaining a reputation in the narcoworld. I heard about only one Juárez narcotrafficker, nicknamed "El Greñas," who was reputed to have given money to help his colonia (Colonia Hidalgo). Said one youth respondent at one of Jorge's youth project areas, "Those stories [about narcotraffickers who do things for the community] are from Durango, Casa Grande, in southern states, Sinaloa. Here in Juárez, who knows?" Said another, "Where I was born there are narcotraffickers that do schools, they do everything. I do not think in Juárez they do, because they say that there are more drugs here than on the other side."

However, even with respect to the south-of-the-border *pueblitos* (villages), respondents characterized narcotraffickers as primarily giving out a lot of money to help their villages, their families, and, in general, those around them, while selling drugs and causing destruction in the next village (or, as one respondent in a group discussion in El Paso put it, while "screwing their race"). Yet even so, when well-known narcocorrido bands performed in the El Paso/Juárez area during the research period, they played to large audiences, either at the Civic Center or an outdoor arena.

Still, even in Juárez (more so, based on discussions and interview responses thus far, than in El Paso) the image of narcotraffickers referred to above coexists with a number of commonly cited folktales and gossip items about narcotraffickers who have near-mythical status throughout Mexico. One of these is the story of Caro Quintero (famous in the 1980s, he is perhaps the prototype of the recent crop of "mega-narcotraffickers" in Mexico), who made a famous declaration from jail in the 1980s that he could pay off Mexico's massive external debt with his wealth. Another is the story (and its many versions) of former Juárez cartel head Amado Carillo Fuentes, called "lord of the skies," who attained a near-mythical reputation for his fleet of airplanes and his ability to appear in one place then another, seemingly at will. There are people who still think that Amado Carillo faked his 1997 death in order to live life as he wanted, free from the constant danger and precariousness of his position as cartel head.

And then there is another entire dimension related to the mythic aspect of the drug trade. I heard various stories (see also Astorga 1997; Kaplan 1998) about a narcotrafficker-saint (El Narcosanto),[7] to which there is a popular shrine in Culiacán, in the state of Sinaloa. The narcosaint is named Jesús Malverde, and, depending upon the source, is said to be a Sinaloan "*bandido generoso*" (generous bandit) who robbed the rich and gave to the poor during the rule of Porfirio Díaz (Astorga 1997; Quiñones 2001b), or a tailor, or a construction worker, or a composite legend, or other things. His exact connection to the drug trade is not clear; nevertheless, his shrine is commonly viewed as a "poor people's shrine," and people who visit it often leave mementos or flowers. He is the "Angel of the Poor" (Quiñones 2001b).

Hearing about El Narcosanto, though, and running into it are different matters. In the Juárez prison—which is on the outskirts of the city, next to dry, dusty, and poverty-ridden Colonia Revolución— I interviewed three men who were convicted of drug trafficking. These three, coincidentally, had formed a corrido group either before they were arrested or while in prison. In any case, the prison director let them keep their instruments—bass violin, accordion, and guitar—and allowed them to bring their instruments to the small staff kitchen and do a show (see Plate 6). Although the kitchen staff acted as if they had seen the group perform before, this seemed unusual to me, certainly not something one would see in a U.S. prison, especially with inmates locked up for a comparable offense. And, these corridistas wore street clothes—hats, boots, belts, jeans, western shirts—not prison garb. They were quite good, as good as anyone I heard on CDs or the radio. They sang several narcocorridos as well as corridos they had written about life in prison. As I listened, I saw that the lead singer wore a large pendant bearing a photo or picture (Plate 7). I asked him who it was. "El Narcosanto," he said in a matter-of-fact manner. Then he spoke briefly about his faith in El Narcosanto—as I interpreted it, not faith so much in a formal religious sense, but a more instrumental faith in the protective powers of the saint, as something that would keep him from harm.

The message that seems to come through is that popular sentiments about narcotraffickers as heroes are complex, perhaps, in some ways, more complex than the common position taken by commentators. James Nicolopulos explains this position as follows (in Wald 1998): "The people who buy these records are very poor, and are struggling under a system which is devised to keep them marginalized. . . . These people who beat the system, who break out of that, are looked upon as culture heroes. There's also the element of conflict with Anglo-Saxon civilization, which is a long running theme in American culture. Because the United States is so intrusive into Mexico in terms of drug policy, if you beat the system, you're also beating the cultural antagonist."

Adult and older respondents who were not recent immigrants or who had more education in their background than most recent immigrants tended to shake their heads and, with some gravity, deplore the way in which the corrido tradition has been "cheapened" by the narcocorridos. To these respondents, the narcocorri-

Plate 6. Norteño group composed of inmates at the Juárez central jail, playing corridos in the employee kitchen.

dos are nothing like the old corridos about revolutionary heroes or figures like Pancho Villa. The primary value underlying narcocorridos, they said, was money. At the same time, several of these respondents acknowledged that "poor people" view narcotraffickers and the money they are able to distribute as a "dream," particularly because most narcotraffickers also come from a background of poverty. Some cited the devaluation of the peso as one factor increasing the gap between rich and poor and increasing the appeal of narcotraffickers as models. Yet there is much hypocrisy, said one respondent, who himself had worked in a maquila, gone to school to get a college degree, then started his own business—a business, now located in El Paso, that sells parts and supplies to the maquilas. To him, narcocorridos represented an effort to cash in on the opening of the Latino market (just as Coca-Cola and other corporations are doing) and on popular reactions to poverty—an exploitation of popular sentiment even while those who create these narcocorridos in turn make substantial amounts of money. El Paso and Juárez were not centers of the drug trade until the 1960s, he said, and then

Plate 7. Corrido musician showing the narcosaint image he wears around his neck.

it got out of hand, due to the demand from the United States. Mexicans have a long-standing tradition against the use of drugs. It is also the case, said this respondent, that the form of the corrido itself plays to the tragic hero character, thus channeling the subject matter accordingly.

This critical view has had a strong proponent in Mexican essayist Carlos Monsiváis, who calls drug trafficking a "disgrace" to Latin America and refutes, vehemently, the portrayal of narcotraffickers as heroes or social bandits (León and Bedoya 1983): "Y no se trata de un bandido social, sino de un delincuente que no tiene la menor intención de distribuir sus ingresos. No es Robin Hood. Es un asesino. El tipo tiene ahora 30 años, y es el mejor ejemplo de cómo lograr una rápida vía de acceso al dinero." Narcotraffickers, says Monsiváis, are not Robin Hoods, but assassins who have no intention of distributing their income. Yet they are a major source of employment and have become examples for how to make money quickly.

The image of the narcotrafficker as described by listeners becomes much more interesting when seen in light of what producers had to say about what goes into creation of the image (see below).

Interpreting Narcocorridos as Inevitable Tragedy

The question of narcocorridos as inevitable tragedies first came up in an interview with a recording industry respondent who cautioned that one should not take out of context the scenarios presented in narcocorridos, because the corrido form itself, at least, this genre of corrido, focuses on misfortunes or death as part of the narrative structure through which the protagonist is represented, and interpreted, as a hero.[8] This view is related to the abovementioned notion of corridos as a "marked genre" and is a very interesting ontological element of corridos that may have some ties, I believe, to ontological elements of other musical or aesthetic genres that grow out of situations of concentrated or recurring poverty, where the life, the character, of the protagonist (in this case, the narcotrafficker) is created, or at least defined, by his or her death. As such, death is part of the developmental process, and the "life" of the protagonist achieves a kind of completeness after death, as an ongoing iteration of a moral type. If this is so, the process also bears some likeness to what anthropologist Victor Turner (1974) has described (with respect to Miguel Hidalgo, father of Mexican independence) as the model of the *via crucis*—the inevitable, and even required, suffering of Mexican cultural heroes, often through betrayal—a model that is "presented by history" to emerging cultural figures in a way that channels its own fulfillment. In any case, this bears further investigation.

Moreover, as will be discussed further, the connection between the narcotrafficker persona and death or tragedy has significant implications in terms of understanding the meaning of actions that may otherwise be perceived as dangerous and destructive. In an applied context, it has many implications with respect to the public health discourse on risk behavior.

The connection between corridos (and narcocorridos) and death is clearly a strong undercurrent. Members of one norteño group told me that, because a corrido is a memorial, it should never be written about someone who is alive; if it is, no name should be mentioned. In fact, a man they knew who was a well-liked community figure, and a narcotrafficker, had a corrido written about him while he was alive. Sure enough, said the group members, he was shot a few months later. They were then called on to write and perform a corrido about him post mortem. Yet this sentiment is clearly not universal, since there are many narcocorridos written about those who are living.

Interpreting Corridos as Moral Lessons

To the outsider, the corrido as a moral lesson may seem an unlikely outcome, given the subject matter. But (as noted earlier) it is not uncommon for narcocorridos to contain a warning about the consequences of involvement in trafficking. Members of Plata Norte said that some of the lyrics address moral issues that have meaning beyond their drug context. For example, there is a corrido about a man who was so involved in the drug business—a kind of workaholic—that he forgot to feed his children. The corrido describes his children in the back of his truck eating cocaine because they were starving as a result of his neglect. It is a narcocorrido, but also a statement about being a responsible parent in this interpretation.

Interpreting Corridos as Jests

Another way in which narcocorridos may be interpreted is as a form of "intercultural jest" (Paredes 1993). Such jests are called "*tallas,*" according to Paredes (Paredes 1993). One form Paredes documented is the *curandero* (folk healer) belief tale. In tallas, American doctors are shown up by a curandero who, after the doctors pronounce the patient incurable, is easily able to cure him or her with a simple remedy of herbs, specific rituals, washing in a certain well or spring, or the like. When the doctors approach the curandero to find out how he did it, the curandero tells them nothing other than a pious "God cured him, not I." The doctors then leave, mystified.

Another kind of joking tradition that narcocorridos may draw from is known as *"relajo,"* described by Barriga (1997, p. 45, quoting Portilla 1966, p. 25) as "a joking relationship that involves a suspension of seriousness that undercuts normative values." It often involves themes of class or social stratification.

With this in mind, there are a number of narcocorridos that make a jest of tricking, evading, or otherwise showing up the Migra, Mexican or U.S. police, or other officials. For example, the corrido "Las Tres Monjas" (The Three Nuns, performed by Exterminador) tells the story of narcotraffickers who dressed up as nuns to transport their drugs across the border. (They were eventually discovered, but then pulled their cuernos out of their habits and engaged in a gunfight.) This is a popular topic for song in general. I also heard, for example, about a song by Vicente Fernández in which he jokes about dying his hair blond to get past the Migra. There are also "self-jests." One that comes to mind is a corrido about the cell phone, making sport of its image as a sign of prestige or of someone who has important things to do.

Several of the youth interviewed, in fact, said that they look at narcocorrido lyrics as fun, or as funny, in the manner of cartoon action or professional wrestling. The narcotrafficker character here is not interpreted as real, but as a fantasy and entertainment— though still drawing on resonant themes. Norteño musicians in Plata Norte said that they themselves listen to narcocorridos along with other norteño music, in part because "we get a kick out of the lyrics," according to one member.

Interpreting Narcocorridos as Image Enhancer and Source of Power

Many sources describe narcocorridos as *"canciones fuertes"* (strong or controversial songs). Even more, they claim that playing narcocorridos helps in the creation of a self-image that is more powerful than the person doing the creating may actually be. Narcocorridos, said sources from Plata Norte, "portray you as an image either that you want others to believe or that you want to believe." By having them around, and playing them, "other people will give you credit for being stronger than you are, more powerful than you are." Thus, it is said that narcocorridos "make you braver, make you stronger." In this way, they function like an intoxicant of power. A gathering of men listening to narcocorridos and drinking alcohol will get "pumped up."

In a sense, this aspect of narcocorridos is similar to the effect that corridos had as songs of the Mexican Revolution and, for that matter, as songs of the Chicano movement in the United States. One source told me, for example, that when he was in prison, Latino inmates sang corridos from the Chicano movement as a source of group solidarity and strength.

Interpreting Narcocorridos as "Country Music" or Lower-Class Music

For many respondents, corridos were clearly a regional signifier, an urban-rural signifier, and a class signifier. This is the sense in which they are listened to for the music as much as the lyrics. The obverse of the positive rural signification for listeners in this category, though, is the negative connotation attached by others to the same signification. Echoing an opinion heard from a number of adults, a middle-aged woman and mother of several children who ran a small restaurant in downtown Juárez said that narcocorridos, and corridos in general, were music that appealed to people with lower levels of education, or to maquila workers. She said that she loved the beautiful norteño romantic ballads, but as for corridos, "they [corrido singers] sing like they are squeezing their necks." And, as mentioned earlier, executives who manage the Juárez radio stations that play corridos and narcocorridos clearly view the music as lower class.

Producer Interpretations and the Role of Mass Media

Perhaps the most striking finding of this study so far has to do with the way in which narcocorridos, a variation on a traditional folk music form, have intersected with the world of mass-media production and distribution. This has, in my view, substantially affected the meaning and role of these corridos vis-à-vis the traditional corrido and has converted a deeply embedded folk idiom into a market niche product, a commodity. In short, traditional, or "classic," corridos were not a mass-media product; narcocorridos—and the narcotrafficker persona they portray—are very much a mass-media product. The way narcocorridos are presented, marketed, and distributed is directly tied to market considerations and to the general imperatives of the mass-media industry.

Interview respondents at EMI-Latin, a major record company

with offices in Los Angeles, generally felt that narcocorridos were "pueblo music," music that appeals primarily to low-income rural people and immigrants from Mexico (or in Mexico). In the United States, they are popular primarily in California, Arizona, Texas, and New Mexico, as well as cities elsewhere, such as Chicago, where there is a large Mexican American population. At the same time, some of the major narcocorrido groups—Los Tucanes de Tijuana and Los Tigres del Norte, in particular—have developed a crossover following both in the United States and throughout Latin America. Los Tucanes, for example, has a gold record in Chile.

The music comes from rural Mexico, and that in large part is what it signifies, though there is general agreement that these corridos and norteño music in general have made inroads among urban populations. Said one industry respondent, "It was 'lower-class' music, but it has exploded in the past five years. It's now in the cities . . . and even in the way people dress." The change came about, according to this respondent, because of a general lack of originality in other Latino pop music forms over the past few years; the genre was getting stale.

Along with the growing popularity of narcocorridos/norteño music, other Latino pop singers like Alejandro Fernández are "returning to the old stuff." In the United States, the burgeoning immigrant population has driven the increase in popularity, particularly since their purchasing power is greater here than it is in Mexico. At the same time, industry respondents noted that as Los Tucanes becomes more popular with a broad audience, the group is playing fewer narcocorridos and more ballads and romantic pop songs. This is worth noting, because it says something about the semiotics of the narcocorrido genre, the "outsider" or rebel position that it symbolizes.

According to industry respondents, the narcotrafficker image in narcocorridos touches a certain double standard in listeners. On the one hand, they know that the drug world portrayed is bad. On the other hand, listening to these "tales" is, said one respondent, "a way to feel better, to be a person of importance . . . a lot of people listening to these want to escape from poverty, and so they imagine." At the same time, the narcocorridos don't always glamorize the drug world. There is, as noted earlier, a message of "live by the sword, die by the sword."

There is another interesting twist: traditional corridos were songs about someone, and while this is still largely true with narcocorridos, they are increasingly about the performer as well. This is not entirely surprising, since they are mass marketed and the per-

formers take on star status. Thus Chalino Sánchez, the first star of
the narcocorrido genre, is himself viewed widely as a hero (every
respondent who talked about Chalino said essentially the same
thing). He is the Pancho Villa of Sinaloa (his home state, and almost
a state-cum-metaphor for the image of the narcotrafficker); indeed,
he recorded a tape of songs entitled "Corridos Villistas." Said one
industry respondent, "He was a rebel, with or without a cause. He
had everything but was willing to risk it anyway." Not only that, he
retained his identity with the migrants and common people. He became rich, but "never left the ranch, never left his people." Listeners
hear about Chalino and hear his music and say, "This is what I want
to be." His is an in-your-face persona, unapologetic about who he
is, in terms of both his ethnicity and his rural roots.

Industry respondents also repeated what listeners said about narcocorrido lyrics, that "they are about what is happening." Los Tucanes de Tijuana have said, "We read the newspaper and write about
what is." But the lyrics are also seen as "outspoken," about drugs,
the United States, the Mexican government, or whomever. They
are marketed as "corridos fuertes" (strong or controversial corridos)
or "*corridos prohibidos*" (prohibited corridos) to signal this image.
As such, they are admittedly marketed very much the same way
as rap and hip-hop have often been marketed, as a no-holds-barred,
in-your-face kind of representation or statement. This parallels, according to one respondent, the direction of Mexican and Latino
television programming, particularly in the United States, in which
"stronger language and themes" have been "seeping in."

Combining the comments of these industry respondents, we can
say that corridos are viewed as representing a kind of openness
about daily reality, harsh or not. Because they are open in this way,
they are, as one respondent noted, a symbol of strength and a break
from tradition. In this they are quite the opposite of traditional
corridos.

Mirroring what was said by several in the listener sample, industry respondents also noted that narcocorrido lyrics were, on occasion, satirical as well, in the manner of a "musical comic strip," full
of wordplay. Again, Los Tucanes' "Mis Tres Animales" was cited as
an exemplar of this type of narcocorrido. These are, in a way, "the
equivalent of Jay Leno or David Letterman."

A Tale of Two Cities

One set of producer interviews, along with a site visit, was conducted with staff of a small narcocorrido recording and producing

company in a predominantly Latino barrio near Long Beach, California. I describe this almost as a case study because it is highly illuminating in terms of the way in which the narcotrafficker image is created and represented in the popularized narcocorrido genre, and in terms of aspects of the music and media business itself which have contributed to the image. It is worth noting that I contacted this company for interviews because I had purchased a number of narcocorrido cassettes in Tijuana and elsewhere that bore their name as producer and recorder, so their products had a reasonable reach for a small company.

The company is a three-generation operation founded by the father, who emigrated some time ago from the Mexican state of Sonora. The sons and daughters and grandchildren all have roles in the business. Two of the sons, along with the father, write narcocorrido lyrics for a stable of norteño bands that they find through various channels. Both brothers also have narcocorrido groups themselves, one of which has apparently received serious airplay and notice from larger recording studios. The sister acts as business manager, and she is a singer in a narcocorrido band of her own. They have a recording studio upstairs, and they produce and duplicate the tapes and CDs. They publish the music, develop the image through which their tapes and CDs are marketed, do all the photography themselves, and handle distribution. This is where the grandchildren fit in. When I was there, two of them, who looked to be about twelve or thirteen, were working in a large room sorting and packing boxes of tapes. In fact, they pointed out with some humor (and to my surprise) that most of the people appearing on the covers of their products are family members dressed up to look like narcotraffickers. There is one tape on which the father appears as a kind of narcocartel elder, brandishing an AK-47. This is the same father who, as I talked with him, was genial, hospitable, and proud that his business was gaining enough of a reputation that someone was coming to study them. And I was not the first; journalist Sam Quiñones had already been there quite a few times. The cover images are generally very explicit in their portrayal of drug deals, drugs, and guns. And the photos are often taken right out in front of the company's small office, then touched up with different background scenes.

The path from the father's emigration to the business today is a story, or perhaps an allegory. The father had some skills, including photography, that he tried to parlay into work when he arrived in the Los Angeles area. Sometimes, he would go to small cantinas where norteño bands were playing and try to take photos of them (for money). Eventually, he offered to record their music, which he and his sons began to do, learning how as they went. At the same time, the family regularly ran a vendor booth at the Paramount, California, swap meet, where they sold cassettes and other items. It was here, in the mid-1980s, that they met Chalino Sánchez, who, at that time, was trying to peddle tapes of his own music. They ultimately became an early distributor of some of Chalino's material, thereby gaining a certain reputation because of his eventual success.

As part of their efforts with local norteño bands and other bands coming up from Mexico, they were also trying to market the music to local radio stations for airplay. But they were, said the sister, constantly rebuffed and told that the music was "low-class, underground music." "We were humiliated, treated badly," she said. At the same time, radio stations were increasingly dominated by large recording companies, which often had the resources, said family members, to bribe radio stations and get their music played. Radio stations themselves were "owned by rich white people, who let the Mexicans run it."

Eventually, the family became angry and frustrated at trying to "beat the business" and decided that they would find a way to compete and survive however they could. As a competitive strategy, they drew from the experience of rap and hip-hop and began to "focus on the bad stuff" (see Ro 1996). They took out ads and created an image for their products (and themselves) that was "on the edge." It was their view that to push through and succeed in the business, it was necessary to build a reputation. "Once you have a reputation, you can do whatever." Developing and maintaining their reputation is also a task of another sort: one of the brothers and the sister who had corrido bands both made it clear that they were not afraid to fight. The sister told me about how, during one performance where someone in the audience was trying to grab the microphone, she had no compunction about hitting or kicking him to prevent him from doing so. The brother said, "We have the guts to do [illegal things], but our father wouldn't allow it."

There was clearly a certain rebel element in their tactics and attitude in response to a pattern of exclusion and stratification in the music and media industry that mirrors, in some ways, larger patterns of social exclusion with respect to Latinos (more specifically, rural, poor Latino migrants). In this way, their own experience is paradigmatic and matches the attitudes and experiences conveyed in narcocorridos: they "live what they do." Speaking rhetorically as if to the dominant media powers, one brother said, defiantly, "Who

are you to stop me!?" And in an explicit acknowledgment of the social symbolism loosely associated with the music, he said, "We're
here to make money and live. I'm sorry I don't have a college education, but I live fine."

There is another level at which the music they produce intersects with other social forces. The lyrics they write, and thus the
core of the image they (and others like them) are supporting, are
not in fact lyrics drawn simply from what "is." They are a combination of multiple cultural influences, daily realities, and a certain
ironic manipulation of the corrido form. The lyrics are, said one
brother, influenced by the presentations of rap and hip-hop artists
like Tupac Shakur, in combination with traditional corrido themes
and formats. But, and very important, they are also influenced by
narcotraffickers themselves. At least since Chalino, traffickers have
regularly contacted and hired norteño bands to write corridos about
them. Once the company began to develop a reputation for recording, writing, producing, and distributing narcocorridos, it was increasingly contacted by, as they put it, "cartel members" to write
corridos for them. From their description, this became a circus of
sorts. Cartel or trafficker representative A would call and request a
corrido. The company would write it and would receive gifts (expensive wines, money) from this source. Then another, perhaps competing, narcotrafficker representative, B, would call and, on occasion, complain or express anger that nothing was being written
about them, and why was it that the company wrote such-and-such
about cartel A. So they would write about cartel B. And so on.

This is not a unique situation. From discussions with musicians
and others familiar with "the narcocorrido scene," I have determined that the connection between narcotraffickers and the production of corridos is, or at least has been, common. In Mexico,
especially in the narcotrafficking heartland of Sinaloa, producing
corridos for money is a popular industry, with newspaper advertise-
ments offering buyers a corrido about themselves for three thousand pesos (see Rivera 1998).

Eventually, the interplay between traffickers became dangerous,
not only because they were caught in the middle between competing traffickers, but also, said one brother, because the U.S. Drug
Enforcement Agency was apparently picking up significant details
and clues from these and other corridos, information which was
used to make arrests or raids. Eventually, they began receiving calls
from these same sources asking them not to write anything about
them in detail, at least not so openly. They now write more "generic" lyrics, taken from what they see in the newspapers, focus-

ing on portrayals of "smaller" characters. But, said the brother, "I could tell you more." And despite the opacity and generic nature of the more recent lyrics, he hinted that those who are well connected "will know." (This was perhaps a boast, and part of his presentation to me as outsider, though it is hard to know.)

Still another level comes into play. While larger record companies and media organizations, for the most part, have shunned the narcocorrido genre (except for a few well-known groups like Los Tucanes), it is likely that they cannot ignore their popularity in the U.S. (and Mexican) Latino market. In Los Angeles, on radio stations such as 105.5 KVUE, and at popular clubs like El Farallón and El Parral, narcocorridos are wildly popular. Los Tucanes first received airplay in Los Angeles and went on to become the "fastest Latino group to go platinum" (interviews with staff of Cintas Acuario, December 1998). (One of the company's artists, Voces del Río, is beginning to get airplay now.) The larger companies, in order to keep up with the market, may have to appropriate the trend, to some extent. In addition, company members said that radio station representatives from, for example, Chicago, where there is a substantial Latino/Mexican market, come to Los Angeles to see what is current. They find out what is on the radio and try to access groups that are popular in the clubs and on the radio. From Los Angeles, then, the influence spreads, driven by the market.

Younger people, according to the sister, look up to narcotrafficker characters because they often started out poor, with nothing, like them. It is a rags-to-riches theme that resonates widely. Indeed, one of the narcocorrido compilations put out by the company is called "De Peones a Reyes . . ." (From Rags to Riches . . .). Young people (and not-so-young people) listen and imagine that they are the dealer in the song and that they, too, can live a life like that.

Yet there are, she said, also many songs about death. This is true of rap and hip-hop as well. In particular, there are songs about a "good death," as in Tupac Shakur's "If I Die When High," and songs about the inevitability of death. In one small cantina, I listened to a corrido on the jukebox in which the corridista first sang about his clothes, his hat, his rings, followed by an explanation that the clothes were not just for show, but for business, followed by a request that listeners "get out their drugs," finally followed by a discussion of death. "Death follows me like a shadow," he sang, and "when I die, bury me in my sweet Durango."

In contrast to what has been said about the traditional corrido, women are an important and growing audience for narcocorridos, according to the sister. If true, this emerges as a change from the

male-gendered world of corrido performance (though not necessarily of corrido subject) described by McDowell (1981, p. 71), when
he wrote that "the corrido, with its propositional content drawn
from the heroic world view, belongs primarily to men. Thus it reflects the large-scale allocation of men and women to separate material and symbolic spheres." Yet there was a recent narcocorrido
about a young woman named Baltazar that was "ridiculously popular" among girls who want to live the lifestyle portrayed. And the
sister (from the Long Beach studio) recently wrote a corrido about
the daughter of a dealer. Instead of going through her traditional
quinceañera, or "coming out" party at age fifteen, this girl got a cell
phone and a truck and took over the drug-dealing business from
her father. The song, one of the first narcocorridos about women,
became popular, and young women started naming themselves "la
chaca" after the character, imagining themselves as that girl and
cheering wildly when the song was played at shows.

There is, it is important to note, an element of fun in the performance and listening. Young women (and young men) dress up in
chero garb. The wannabees wear extra gold. The real narcotraffickers are not so gaudy; they are more "professional" (this assessment
directly corroborates the descriptions and assessments described
earlier from youth respondents in Juárez). But, noted the sister, the
fad of dressing up as a chero is fading, replaced by chains, Nike
warm-ups, and other clothing more characteristic of the gangsta rap
look. This is interesting, because it points to the transcultural merg-
ing of rap/hip-hop and narcocorrido signification and semiotics.

How does this family respond to the charges that their music
promotes negative and criminal behavior? As hypocritical, especially coming from the very large corporations that control and
bribe radio stations. They feel some guilt, but feel that "if you raise
your children right," it won't be a problem.

Listening and Doing: Narcocorridos and Individual Action

Very few interview respondents directly attributed to narcocorridos per se any "risk behavior" (to use the term common in behavioral science discourse in reference to drug-related activities, violence, and other health-risk activities) that they were or had been
involved in, or specific risk behaviors of others. This is to be expected. It is typically difficult to make such direct links between the
consumption of an image and some "output" of behavior, because
there are too many mediating factors. Moreover, there are many listeners who assume the narcotrafficker image, and even style them-

selves that way, but who are not in fact involved in drug use, sales, or violence. I interpret this as almost a form of sympathetic magic, in which a person wears the clothing of or acts like a particular figure with the hope of drawing from, or using, what the character represents.

Nevertheless, as mentioned earlier, narcocorridos are part of a lived-in world that includes the world of narcotraffickers, the world of people from the pueblo or from the working class, and a media-created world disseminated through mass-media outlets. Interview and observation data, however, suggest where connections may exist between image consumption and action. Several field observations are pertinent.

At the Los Tigres concert in El Paso, I stood outside for some time, watching the stream of people who came to the show. Because Los Tigres has been around for a long time and are generally well known, the audience was varied in age and style (for lack of a better word). However, most attendees came in chero dress to some degree or other, and there was a subset of this group, mostly younger, who presented themselves as narcotraffickers—if not in reality, at least in style. A number of younger cheros came in with cell phones and/or pagers and small entourages that included women. I saw one young man who, in my interpretation, appeared to take his self-presentation very seriously: he was dressed in chero style, but "with an edge," as one might say. In addition to the usual chero-style elements, he wore a black hat and a long black coat. His face jutted out, his eyes were like slits. He barely looked at the ticket taker as he went through the turnstile. There was little question that his image was of someone not to be messed with. To sum up, the Tigres show was, among other things, an arena were some narcotraffickers and narcotrafficker wannabees could, essentially, display themselves. These are of course my observations and my interpretations of what I observed.

There are a number of bars in Juárez and El Paso which are known as hangouts for narcotraffickers. At various times, a knowledgeable friend took me to about six of these on both sides of the border. In Juárez, the following scenario was common: although sometimes unremarkable-looking on the outside, the inside of these "narco-bars" was often quite nice—maybe not exactly elegant, but a world apart from the dark, dank, and narrow working-class cantinas in the alleys near the old *mercado* area. In one particular bar, the walls were lime-green tile, with sections of glass tile allowing some light in for something of a fresh or airy feel. In the center was a polished-wood circular bar. Within the center of the circle were not only the bartenders but also a cluster of very sharply dressed bar girls (e.g., one in a tight, very short pin-striped suit; another in a short skirt and halter top, which she kept tying and retying), who, as I understand it, have multiple roles. On the one hand, their job is to make money for the bar. For this their "equipment" is themselves and a chair, which they pull up on the opposite side of the bar from a customer (preferably one who looks like he can spend money). Here they engage the customer in conversation, which stimulates drink buying. It was apparent, and no surprise to me (from body language and action), that they cater to customers who are known as spenders (and who sometimes look the part, with rings, jewelry, etc.). Many of these are also narcotraffickers, who come in and take their places in what amounts to a theater of power, expressed as a sort of commerce in joie de vivre, though with an edge. At one table in the corner, a heavyset man wearing a big black western hat and wraparound sunglasses sat with several others; at the bar, several well-dressed men were engaged in gregarious conversation with the girls. I heard that some of the bar girls also become "girlfriends" of the narcotraffickers who come in — not necessarily as prostitutes in the manner that the term is usually employed, but in an ongoing relationship of some kind. In any case, like the Tigres concert, these bars were clearly a place to be seen, a place for the display of the narcotrafficker persona.

In El Paso, the scene was somewhat different. The two narcobars I went to there did not display as much of a ceremonious apparatus for catering to narcotraffickers as mini-emperors. At the same time, there was still a sense of show. At one bar, three or four men in boots and hats walked in with purposeful strides and headed directly to the end of the bar to converse with the owner, whom they clearly knew. After a brief conversation, they pulled out cell phones and began what certainly appeared like business conversations, though it was impossible to know. In any case, the exact details of the conversation were almost of no importance, because what struck me was the presentation, the appearance of having important things going on.[9] During these conversations, two of the men walked out of the bar and came back in, again with the appearance of a specific purpose for doing so. When I left, I saw their truck—a shiny black four-wheel-drive—which stood out in the dark, seedy parking lot.

What is relevant here, as in the previous example, is the key element of public presentation and "acting as if" within a social arena that is a known setting for becoming, displaying, and maintaining a narcotrafficker persona. Some of these locations may also be frequented by wannabees, who learn the code of presentation through interaction with the scene. They may also cross over to actual involvement at some point.

One day I went in to the Juárez youth prison, a low-profile building of cement and flaking paint, off Boulevard Fronteriza and not far from the border. There is a small entry or waiting area, but, generally, the prison is a fairly grim cement compound with three sections—one for younger boys (mostly about ages ten to fourteen or so), one for older boys who are in for more serious offenses, and one for girls. The boys, including younger boys, sleep in cells, and I mean *cells*. Steel bars. Little light. Cracked cement. Tiny little bed and blanket. There are some rooms that are said to be for school, but these are virtually bereft of anything that looks like educational material. The younger boys have a separate courtyard for playing outdoors, little more than a dirt square. In the older boys' compound, it is much the same. Seven or eight boys (I'm guessing about sixteen to eighteen years old) are playing basketball. My friend and guide Jorge motions me to stay outside as he goes in to talk to a young man who has been locked up for something. The conversation is serious.

Over in the girls' compound, the setup is slightly different. The girls are in small dorm-style rooms, with maybe five to eight girls in a room on spare bunkbeds. Same drab cement, though some of it is painted yellow. About fifteen girls are sitting out in a larger room, watching television. I was told that some of the girls here have been brought in by parents or relatives, apparently for drug use and other behavior that parents could not control. There is a small contingent of shy-looking Tarahumara girls, in for drug-related problems, including the inhaling of an industrial paint thinner that people call *"agua celeste"* (celestial water). I was able to interview a group of younger boys and a few boys in the section for older boys.

All the boys whom I interviewed in the section of the Juárez youth prison for younger offenders, when asked about the image of narcotraffickers in narcocorridos, said that they wanted to be narcotraffickers themselves. Not only that, but they wanted to be the *best* narcotrafficker, not just any narcotrafficker. The qualities they viewed as admirable were those that could be ascribed to successful narcotraffickers, for example, having money, being well dressed, and "not having problems with others," a phrase that, in context, I took to mean the ability to do what you intend. These youth were already incarcerated for what were said to be minor crimes, so narcocorridos may have been for them a validation of goals and values that they already perceived to be meaningful. Simultaneously, the social context of these comments cannot be ignored. In these interviews, I tried to draw out any contrasts between what they admired in narcotraffickers and what they generally felt were admirable qualities and admirable people. I attempted to find out if narcotraffickers were viewed as helping other people, a quality often mentioned as admirable in interviews with youth. But these youth felt, essentially, that there was no one out there who would help people, except for their own family. And in a comment I found disturbing, but not surprising, one youth, with agreement from all the others in this group, said, "If you want to help people, don't be in the government, because they will kill you, like Colosio [referring to the Mexican presidential candidate who was assassinated in 1994], or like Kennedy." Their sense of cynicism, and nihilism of a sort, was well developed even at a young age. Why not, then, be a narcotrafficker? Look at how they live! Look at their lives, so fantastic (as portrayed in some narcocorridos and in the general mythology about them)! And, said the youth, they are famous: "They have corridos written about them."

In an interesting note, however, the two respondents I interviewed in the older boys' section had a different view. They had been involved in drug-trafficking activity, but both expressed a negative opinion of narcotraffickers and the life associated with them. Their opinion could have been an attempt to say what they knew I wanted to hear (because they were older and more savvy about such things). However, it closely resembles opinions about drug dealing that I heard several years ago when conducting a study on street youth. Older adolescents who had been involved in the drug market for a while often wanted to get out, because they had already experienced the downside of the life. This, I believe, was also true at least for the two Juárez youth I interviewed in the older boys' section. One, in fact, specifically mentioned that he held this opinion because the petty dealer he worked for was killed, and he witnessed the killing. He did not want to end up like that.

The connection between narcocorridos, the "celebretization" of narcotraffickers, and involvement in risk behavior may have a different trajectory with young women, though this is evolving. Young women interviewed in one El Paso focus group were already in a gang prevention program, and their involvement in gang activities could hardly be attributed to narcocorridos. However, once again, their attraction to gang activity was probably fed by narcocorridos, along with other media and day-to-day mythology surrounding and celebretizing narcotraffickers (as players). If nothing else, attending norteño music and narcocorrido performances at certain local clubs provided at least one opportunity to "mingle with the players" in a setting where some of the music being performed also validated and foregrounded involvement in trafficking.

Comments from music industry sources (as noted above), however, lead me to believe that there is another dimension with respect to women. Because narcocorridos are a mass-media product, how they are interpreted merges, to some degree, with other mass media in reflecting social changes among Mexican and Latino peoples, including changes concerning the role of women. So, if some narcocorridos are being written and performed about women who are themselves narcotraffickers—not social props, hangers-on, or girlfriends of narcotraffickers—then they present that role as one in which women are powerful and celebretized for that power via the same or similar persona currently gendered for men. If the comments from the music industry source are reliable, the level of enthusiasm about this role among young women in the narcocorrido audience is very high and forms part of an emerging ethos, spurred by the mass media (including narcocorridos) concerning social roles and the open discussion of topics that are controversial and formerly viewed as taboo for discussion, especially by women.

This kind of information, in conjunction with other contextual data, suggests another way to understand the connection between the media images of narcotraffickers and actual practice: the assembling of a semiotics of self to give coherence to behavior already engaged in, a process which may in turn shape behavior as well in a kind of circular, self-reinforcing process. (This is discussed more fully in reference to the mechanism of the persona in Chapter 4.)

There were, however, a few instances when respondents did link narcocorridos specifically to involvement in drug trafficking or other such actions. This was, interestingly, limited (by respondents) to the Mexican side. They said that in Juárez, youth who listened to narcocorridos formed an impression that drug trafficking was an easy thing, particularly in Mexico, where police were viewed as corrupt and where, even in jail, narcotraffickers with money bribed officials and set up luxurious jail cells with television sets and other amenities. That impression was enough (so it was said) to encourage some youth to try getting involved. In such cases, the narcocorridos appear to serve as both enticement and "road map"—the latter because of their often-detailed descriptions of the narcotrafficking life. Members of Plata Norte also felt that narcocorridos were an influence, because of the life they portray, which is so different from the life of many of their listeners, and hence so attractive.

4. Narcocorridos and the Cultural Persona of the Narcotrafficker

A Culturally "Shaped" Response to Social Stratification?

Using the data summarized in the previous chapter, we can now return to the research questions and draw some preliminary conclusions. First, are narcocorridos, and the narcotrafficker (narco) persona they feature, primarily a genre of representation that has arisen out of the world of the subaltern, the dispossessed, and the poor within a framework of social stratification? The answer to the question is a mixed *yes and no*. It would be easy to essentialize narcocorridos this way, under a schema wherein they are representations employing a traditional narrative form featuring a cultural persona that symbolizes resistance to the oppression of the class system in Mexico, global capitalism, and the United States (versus Mexico)—that they are at heart oppositional in nature, a discursive point of resistance, a counterdiscourse.

Several scholars of current corridos have made this argument, including Guillermo Hernández (1992), who notes that in most narcocorridos, drugs and drug trafficking are not the primary focus; it is the conflict with authorities and other themes of opposition that are foregrounded (see also Nicolopulos 1997). Along these same lines, Nicolopulos mentions that, in the 1970s, there were a number of corridos about Lucio Cabanas, a schoolteacher who led one of the best-known of several guerrilla movements following the Mexican government's brutal massacre of students in Tlatelolco in 1968, and who was eventually killed by Mexican troops. These corridos were banned by the official (the government's) musician's union. In the 1990s, government authorities in the state of Sinaloa and in other parts of Mexico banned the playing of narcocorridos, lending them a similar antiauthoritarian, counterdiscursive patina.

In Mexico, Luis Astorga (1997) has argued that narcocorridos represent a kind of counterdiscourse against state-controlled media representations of those involved in drug trafficking, a means through which to portray an alternate image. This counterdiscursive image not only targets state representations of drug traffickers, but also is an indigenous construction—and assertion—of a meaningful identity for those in "marginalized social categories," stigmatized from birth.

Based on my data and experience, however, I cannot make this argument unequivocally, much as I might like to. This is not to say that narcocorridos do not have these elements within them, because it is clear to me that the genre does draw, sometimes very powerfully, from such a context. But the picture is more complex than that, and also more interesting, if one can forgive the use of an adjective so abstract and neutral.

Narcocorridos, as a narrative genre drawing from the corrido tradition, are created within a weltanschauung that includes a number of loosely shared or, at least, loosely understood, presuppositions: about antagonism between those in power and the common people; about class and social divisions and solidarities; about national and regional pride; about reputation, bravery, and death; (now) about celebrity and being known; about money and power; and about the special connections between the music, the land (northern Mexico, the border, the sierra), and a concomitant popular identity. Clearly, the issues of power and class are not without ambiguity: there are corridos about political leaders, authorities, and various notables from the ranks of the elite who are perceived as having the people's interests at heart (e.g., Kennedy, Colosio, or even, in some cases, the *federales* who are fighting narcotraffickers; see Ramírez-Pimienta 1998). But corridos, simply put, have not generally been written by the wealthy and powerful to memorialize themselves. (Although, ironically, this has changed with the narcocorrido, because they are utilized to memorialize or flatter narcotraffickers, who may, in fact, be very wealthy.) For narcocorridos, these basic elements remain, at least at the representational level, though, as noted, the realities may be different. Narcotraffickers have been, for the most part,[1] people with low levels of formal education, people from the subaltern strata in Mexican society who have, on occasion, become famous, rich, and powerful—even if only for a short time. And they have done so against a background of poverty, economic instability, and a glaring chasm between rich and poor as well as between the U.S. and Mexican economies. So the basic elements which make up the ecology of the genre are there, and, on the surface, narcocorridos are easily fit into this mold.

The data support this: narcocorridos are primarily viewed as popular among people with less education, rural people, and migrants, even when the songs are listened to by others who do not place themselves in those categories. They are, as noted in the review of the data, also a form of self-assertion by their primary listening population, self-assertion about rural, regional, and subaltern identity. This, by extension, can apply to the world of drugs, drug trafficking, and smuggling as well, because it is well ensconced in the rural culture of many parts of northern Mexico, as exemplified in the title of one popular narcocorrido: "¿Somos Cocodrilos . . . No Hay de Qué?" (basically, "We Are Cokeheads . . . What of It?").

There is a border issue here. An argument could also be made that smuggling, whether of drugs or other contraband, reverses what Kearney (1998) has described as the loss of value that occurs when people migrating across the border from Mexico to the United States become categorized as "illegal aliens," as people without rights, under the stratifying discourse of immigration, which operates at the point of the border. However, when *commodities* are smuggled across the border, they *gain* value because of their legally imposed scarcity, and the smuggling also boosts the value and prestige of those who make it happen, the traffickers. Thus the act of smuggling could be viewed as a kind of commodified, symbolic retribution for the loss in value that is associated with *people* who are migrants or peasants.

Yet narcocorridos are also popular with, or at least known to, a broader audience. In this sense, they are much like rap/hip-hop, which originated on the street, so to speak, but which has become popular with broad audiences, in part because of its appropriation of "hip" and its dominance of the symbolic faddism of rebelliousness, edginess, and danger. The broader popularity of narcocorridos draws from a similar appropriation, though they do not carry quite the "hip cachet" that rap/hip-hop does. In contrast to rap/hip-hop, the broader popularity of narcocorridos also comes from the fact that they are often viewed as clever or humorous—something that can rarely be said about the darker and more aggressive rap/hip-hop genre—and because they are, in form and sound, like other corridos and norteño music, with a resulting general appeal that is regional and class based.

The corrido genre, and therefore the ways in which corrido protagonists are represented and interpreted, is, to some degree, rooted in the turbulent "zone of the imaginary" that is northern Mexico and the border region, both in its real-life conditions and in the way life and values are thought about and portrayed, a certain habitus, if you will. This was true for classic corridos and remains true for contemporary narcocorridos. When corridos like "Gregorio Cortez" first became popular in the mid-nineteenth century, they were bound up in the changing landscape of power between the United States and what had been Mexico, as they were also inextricably bound up with the historical oppositions between the fluidity and independence of the Mexican periphery vis-à-vis the center in Mexico City. They were, and are, also bound up with images of what it means to be from the sierra, or from the tough, dry border country—images of people who are survivors, who are wily and resourceful, who know the land, who can take punishment, and who are not deterred by the imposition of a border. In a 1983 film about Gregorio Cortez,[2] a considerable amount of time is devoted to the chase between the Texas Rangers and Cortez, who manages to outrace, outwit, and generally foil the Rangers' efforts until the very end, when he is finally captured. Cortez prolongs the chase because he knows the land, knows his horse, and has support from people in the villages. He is captured—true to corrido form—only because of the treachery of a fellow Mexican who gives away his hiding place.

Druglord Pablo Acosta, from the Ojinaga area southeast of Juárez, grew up in a family and community near the border in which smuggling (of almost anything, including wax) and the ability to survive in the bone-dry hills was the stuff that gave individuals (primarily men) their reputation in the community (Poppa 1990). In a sense, as a trafficker Acosta simply carried on the tradition, writ slightly larger because of the impact of the drug trade. His reputation was still based on many of the same characteristics.

Furthermore, contemporary narcocorridos are bound up with the persistent fluidity of a reality (in the border region and elsewhere) in which border-obviating population and cultural flows exist in the face of institutionalized state boundaries and boundary policies regarding trade, drugs, immigration, labor, and so on, reinforcing an undercurrent of conflict. They are also bound up with the changing nature and organization of global capital, particularly the transnational utilization of labor. In the Mexican case, this is manifested via the maquilas, which are primarily located on the border, and in the sprawl of colonias populated by so many migrants who come north to find work or some way to scrape out a living. Many of these colonias are, as I have described, scenes of egregious poverty that exists in the face of both maquila-related and drug or contraband money.

What relationship do narcocorridos and the narcotrafficker persona have to these economic conditions? For one, while the maquilas clearly provide income and a means of personal advancement

for some, they also serve as a cauldron, an incubator of an intensi-
fied money struggle, precisely because of the contrast created when
some people benefit while many others benefit only by surviving,
often living in makeshift shelters with few or no services. (But, it
is said, they *are* employed!) More than that, the maquilas, the trade
in drugs and immigrants, and NAFTA-related increases in trade
across the border all foreground the struggle for money in a way
that is tied to longer-term structural configurations of power that
have a lengthy history of framing events and social circumstances
around the border: The United States versus Mexico, elite versus
nonelite, periphery versus center. The struggle for money is symbolically intertwined with these already-existing divisions and conflicts, so that, for a nonelite rural Mexican migrant, making money
is, more and more, immediately and publicly related to where one
is categorized vis-à-vis these other social imperatives and themes.
This was very clear in interviews, whether the respondent favored
or opposed this trend. The fact that the well-known narcotraffickers, and the narcotrafficker image itself, are so entwined with both
money (and all its glitzy by-products) and issues of public power is
not surprising. The fact that narcotraffickers, and the image thereof,
intermingle with the "legitimated" social roles of wealth and power
is not surprising. Neither is the move that situates them, in some
cases, as popular protagonists or even heroes, in corridos and everyday talk. And this is not just directed to Americans, though maquilas are represented as (primarily) American, and it is the American
Immigration and Naturalization Service, Border Patrol, and Drug
Enforcement Administration that stand out as ubiquitous signs of
state force along and near the border. While somewhat ambiguous,
there is thus an element of low-level politics in the narcotrafficker
persona, in the manner described by Scott (1985).

Along this same line, narcocorridos, like any emerging media
product, are bound up in the dominating influence of the market,
under which the "othering" process (the process of assessing and
categorizing population groups as other than oneself) is inseparable
from one's position as buyer or seller, whether the product is drugs
or diapers. The truth of this is amply reflected in the fact that some
"narcocorridos" are not about the drug trade at all, but about the
trade in people, the transport of undocumented people across the
border as big business.

Finally, narcocorridos are bound up in the exploding world of
transnational media, which is a purveyor and shaper of cultural
trends without reference to traditional state borders and, increas-

ingly, both a marketing tool (for narcotraffickers) and just one more potential doorway to wealth. Making and performing narcocorridos now means big money, and the narcotrafficker persona cultivated in narcocorridos is a key part of that. So while narcocorridos are about a constructed world of selling drugs (or people, as the case may be), they are themselves a kind of drug, at least from one angle. Sell drugs, make money, be powerful—no matter what your humble roots may be. Sell narcocorridos, make money, be powerful—no matter what your humble roots. This is a radical departure from what corridos once were. As a further departure and side effect of their integration into the mass media, narcocorridos have also been affected by the changes in gender stereotypes pushed by popular telenovelas and other programs, such that they have not only become popular with women, but there appear to be some narcocorridos which are in fact *about* women—not as girlfriends, but as narcotraffickers themselves (more on this below).

The Narcotrafficker as a Cultural Persona

If narcocorridos are polysemic in their relationship to the socioeconomic setting, what of the narcotraffickers about which they sing? Given the research issues and the historical role of corridos and their protagonists, is the narcotrafficker, as represented in the narcocorridos, a "social bandit" in Hobsbawm's sense? Are narcotraffickers conceptualized as heroes that emerge from the mise-en-scène of poverty and class? Though Hobsbawm (1969, pp. 14–16) views social banditry as a rural and peasant phenomenon that occurs in agrarian economies where there are oppressive conditions for the peasantry, the description can be applied to other situations:

> The point about social bandits is that they are [peasant] outlaws whom the lord and the state regard as criminals, but who remain within [peasant society], and are considered by their people as heroes, as champions, avengers, fighters for justice, perhaps even leaders of liberation, and in any case as men to be admired, helped and supported. . . . It is found in one or other of its three main forms . . . the noble robber or Robin Hood, the primitive resistance fighter or guerrilla unit of what I shall call the haiduks, and possibly also the terror-bringing avenger.

As Hobsbawm (1969) and Herrera-Sobek (1993) note, the "noble robber" may have the following characteristics:

1. The noble robber begins his career of outlawry not by crime, but as the victim of injustice, or through being persecuted by authorities for some act which they, but not the custom of his people, consider criminal.
2. He rights the wrongs.
3. He takes from the rich and gives to the poor.
4. He never kills except in self-defense or to seek a just revenge.
5. If he survives, he returns to his people as an honorable citizen and member of the community. Indeed, he never actually leaves the community.
6. He is admired and supported by his people.
7. He dies invariably through treason, since no decent member of the community would help the authorities against him.
8. He is—at least in theory—invisible and invulnerable.
9. He is not the enemy of the king or emperor, who is the fount of justice, but only of the local gentry, clergy, or other oppressors.

As I outlined earlier, the consensus from interviews was that narcotraffickers do not quite approach the level of social bandits in the popular imagination, though they approach this status to a much higher degree for people who come from the sierra or more rural areas of northern Mexico. In these areas, they are (reputedly) involved in much more of a social role as providers of community support than they are in Juárez or El Paso, where the action revolves much more around showing off, competition for power, and the harsh business of transporting drugs (or other contraband) across the border.

To understand this, I propose thinking in terms of cultural personas or archetypes. Seeking to understand corridos as purveyors of cultural archetypes (I use the term "persona") is not new in itself. From a feminist perspective, Herrera-Sobek (1990) extensively analyzes a number of archetypes recurrent in corridos. In doing so, she, along with others, confronts the problem that the term "archetype," as introduced in psychology by Jung (1959), refers to representations in the unconscious that are related to structures of the psyche, and are therefore fixed. While disagreeing with the inflexibility of the term used this way, Herrera-Sobek and others argue for its utility in analyzing artistic and literary production, which tends to reflect a series of patterns. As amplified below, the concept is also useful for anthropology. To distinguish it from its Jungian usage, however, I use the term "persona."[3] In this usage, the archetype or persona is a culturally constructed, flexible representation existing and dis-seminated over time, embodied as a person and iterations of that person.

Thus we can look briefly at what could be viewed as a "bor-der area" character standard for a social-bandit persona, exempli-fied by Pancho Villa, controversial hero and one of the key, and most popular, military leaders of the Mexican Revolution of 1911. He was known for his gun-toting, no-quarter attitude, but also for giving land to peasants and building schools in the territories he controlled. Like many who were his followers, he was poor (and an orphan), of sharecropper origins, and had little formal educa-tion (Katz 1998). When the United States refused to support him with weapons, he conducted raids into the United States, and then evaded attempts by a U.S. expeditionary force under General Persh-ing to capture him. For this, and for his previous revolutionary ex-ploits, he became a folk hero and subject of many corridos. And, true to the model, he was assassinated in 1923 (Katz 1998; Such-licki 1996).

The Villa and narcotrafficker personas overlap with other popu-larized (and stereotypical) portrayals of the Latino "macho male." According to Mirande (1997; also see Goldwert 1985), the popular-ized character type of the macho male was, after Mexican indepen-dence, introduced into the political arena as the political strongman or caudillo. Porfirio Díaz ruled as an authoritarian, macho figure, and then the Revolution of 1910 unleashed "an orgy of machismo, sexual rampages and destructiveness" (Goldwert 1985, p. 163; Mi-rande 1997). Pancho Villa is often cited as the epitome of this char-acter. Mirande (1997, p. 41) cites Aniceto Aramoni (1965, p. 151), who writes that Pancho Villa exhibited "an extreme, compensatory exaggeration of the personality, narcissism, petulance, aggressive-ness, intense destructiveness, considerable hatred of superiors, . . . a deep contempt for and fear of women." According to Mirande (1997), Villa appealed to the masses because he symbolized a peon, or lower-class person, taking a stand against the dominant classes:

> Mexicans seem to identify vicariously with the person who "bears with it," who is brave, *que no se deja* (who doesn't take anything from anyone), and *que no se raja* (who doesn't back down), especially if the person is depicted as an underdog and of poor or humble origins (citing Aramoni 1965: 163). Villa's invasion of the United States, for example, was celebrated because it demonstrated his audacity in taking on the most powerful nation in the world. In the end, what mattered was

not that the battle was won or lost or that numerous casualties were incurred but that Villa *tenía huevos* (he had "balls") and was man enough to take on the hated yanquis.

And, as mentioned, the narcotrafficker persona overlaps with the image of the tough survivor of the sierra described earlier.

But to place too much weight on an evaluation of the narcotrafficker character against a delineated standard would be to commit an ethnocentric error ascribed by Octavio Paz (1985, pp. 20, 22) to the abstract and sterile nature of North American culture: "the North American, who wanders in an abstract world of machines, fellow citizens and moral precepts . . . [who] wants to use reality rather than to know it." Regardless of how he or she may be exploited in some narcocorridos, the narcotrafficker has become a larger-than-life character, a cultural persona that is a brother (or sister) to the Pancho Villas and many other characters flowing in and out of Mexican culture (which, at the highest level, include legendary or mythical characters such as La Malinche and La Llorona). As such this character exists outside of and beyond the actual lives of any given narcotrafficker. Because of this, when narcocorridos are sung about a particular narcotrafficker, corridistas are singing about that narcotrafficker and *simultaneously* about the narcotrafficker persona. Thus narcocorridos are both contemporary narrative and homage to a transcendent myth. The fact that narcocorridos are not always interpreted in a serious manner does not detract from this, but supports it, because even when they are interpreted as humor, it is my clear sense that they are interpreted in the way Barthes' wrestlers are interpreted (Barthes 1972), as cartoonlike on the one hand, yet as larger-than-life, ritualistic theater on the other. And the fact that the myth is exploited (often cynically and hypocritically) by both narcotraffickers and music and media corporations only supports the vital existence of the myth itself: if it did not have popular power, it could not be exploited.

The narcotrafficker persona is therefore a packed, polysemic symbol much like the mudyi (milk) tree of the Ndembu (Turner 1967). And it is a symbol that was born in the nexus of class, power, national identity, and regional identity, so, realities aside, it retains these traces. Following John Thompson (1995), however, the narcotrafficker persona as symbol is now also a *commodity*, because it is a representation that can be disseminated and used anywhere, via the modern media, without a necessary connection to place and people.

One of the striking characteristics of this narcotrafficker persona, however, dawned on me late in the fieldwork period, after hearing so many times that a person had a corrido written about him or her, ergo, they were famous, or infamous, or important, or even heroic, and after seeing numerous narcocorridos with some verse or stanza about death and the inevitability of death, as well as the ubiquity of treachery. It became clear that the connection between the co-rrido and the persona is probably organic and provides a dividing line between the two realms in which the narcotrafficker persona lives—the living and the dead. In fact, it may be the case that the narcotrafficker persona is not complete unless he or she has been betrayed or is dead. Thus, as noted in discussion of the data, death is an ontological stage in the completion of this character. The character, at its fullest, must live as if he or she is willing to risk all, then suffer a great tragedy or die a dramatic death, going out with guns blazing. Then, the character continues to live as the subject matter of corridos. One is necessary for the other.

There are many cultural antecedents for this. Octavio Paz (1985, p. 54), writing on the role of death in Mexican culture, explains that "our deaths illuminate our lives." And directly apposite to corridos, he speaks of death as a reflection, as a summation of life: "Tell me how you die and I will tell you who you are" (p. 54). Thus corridos are often tales of how someone died, as a way of saying who they were, as well as of conveying an ongoing message, like a historico-cultural chain letter, about how to be.

In this, narcocorridos are not unique. Other tales and legends of heroes around the world often follow a similar pattern. As Bauman (1986, p. 140),[4] for example, has described them, the *sturlunga sagas* of Iceland are myths or poems, recited publicly, that "celebrate ex-emplary behavior," particularly "*drengskapr* . . . the cover term for the ideal complex of manly virtue and honor." Icelanders, at the time, were said to be obsessed with honor, esteem, and reputation, in much the same way that such arguments have been made about Mexicans. And the honor of a given individual "had to be publicly acknowledged, by being talked about and evaluated" through the public narrative. And certainly other literary heroes have been ful-filled as dramatic characters in death.

Furthermore, as noted previously in this book, corridos in general, as well as narcocorridos, are selective discourse—selecting for the aspects of events and protagonists that contain conflict, drama, and the potential for death. So, the form of the persona is in part shaped by the nature of the form, though, from the opposite direction, the character of the persona may be, by its own nature, a good fit for corridos.

The Narcotrafficker Persona and Changing Gender Roles

While I have discussed the narcotrafficker persona primarily as a male character, I encountered strong indications that this is changing, at least in some small way. As mentioned previously, there are narcocorridos out there about women as narcotraffickers, not just as girlfriends. This change, according to some respondents, parallels changes in the way other popular media (primarily television) have been portraying women and, in general, how the Spanish-language media have been openly discussing subject matter that was formerly taboo.

Representations Encapsulated within the Narcotrafficker Persona

Thus, to summarize, it could be argued that the narcotrafficker persona is one current iteration of a Mexican (and transcultural) persona that, as a packed symbol, represents, in Mexico and among Mexican immigrants, something like the following, set out against a structure of stratification:

For Elite and Middle-class Strata
  A. Power and status achieved "outside the rules"; therefore, a form of rebellion and abandon vis-à-vis "traditional values"; and
  B. Degeneration of values.

Across Strata
  A. Representations of masculinity and (male-gendered) power widely disseminated in Mexican culture;
  B. Representations related to long-standing U.S.-Mexico conflict—as a person who stands in opposition to U.S. power, who is able to "defeat" U.S. power, and who brings to light contradictions in U.S. policy;
  C. Widely shared cultural understandings about boundaries between life and death, and the presence of life after death; and
  D. For a small (but growing) subset of narcocorridos in which the narcotrafficker is female, power and status achieved "outside the rules"; therefore (again), a form of rebellion and abandon vis-à-vis traditional values.

For Subaltern Strata
  A. Reversal of the common circumstance—representation of an individual who has gained power and status without

Representing . . .   **Perpetuated and evolved through . . .**

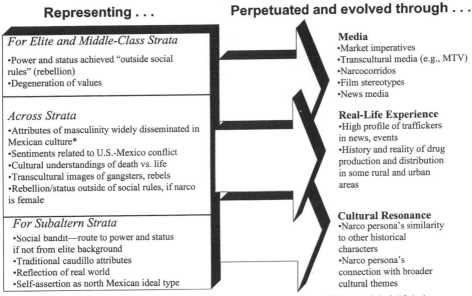

For Elite and Middle-Class Strata

•Power and status achieved "outside social rules" (rebellion)
•Degeneration of values

Across Strata

•Attributes of masculinity widely disseminated in Mexican culture*
•Sentiments related to U.S.-Mexico conflict
•Cultural understandings of death vs. life
•Transcultural images of gangsters, rebels
•Rebellion/status outside of social rules, if narco is female

For Subaltern Strata

•Social bandit—route to power and status if not from elite background
•Traditional caudillo attributes
•Reflection of real world
•Self-assertion as north Mexican ideal type

Media
•Market imperatives
•Transcultural media (e.g., MTV)
•Narcocorridos
•Film stereotypes
•News media

Real-Life Experience
•High profile of traffickers in news, events
•History and reality of drug production and distribution in some rural and urban areas

Cultural Resonance
•Narco persona's similarity to other historical characters
•Narco persona's connection with broader cultural themes

Note: "'Disseminated" means these understandings are *known* to many. Actual practice and concurrence with these popularized attributes have been shown to vary.

Figure 1. The Narcotrafficker Persona

   coming from an elite or dominant background, who provides for "his people"; the social bandit syndrome;
B. Foregrounding of the common circumstance—fame given to a traditional, rural "big man" or caudillo;
C. Foregrounding of the common circumstance—reflection of the real world of drug dealing, violence that exists on the street; and
D. Self-assertion—of a clever and tough northern Mexican ideal type.

Figure 1 depicts this framework and how it is perpetuated.

Theoretical Implications of the Cultural Persona

Cultural Personas as "Thick" Symbols

The existence of the narcotrafficker as persona suggests a number of possible implications, with respect to both theory and applied work. First, the narcotrafficker persona is just one persona, disseminated to a broad public via corridos and, now, other popular media. Could it be said that other such culturally grounded personas exist as well, and that, generally speaking, these kinds of transcendent personas are one important symbolic vehicle through which cultural understandings exist (as "bundles" or nodes) over time, evolve over time, are contested, and are disseminated to a broader population? Or that the loose sets of representations, understandings, and practices referred to as "culture" are embodied in groupings of character archetypes or personas? What I mean, speaking crudely, is that for a given cultural field (a given culture x), is there some inventory of personas, each of which is a symbolic aggregate of a subset of the various understandings or representations that exist as part of that culture, including those that are in conflict or even opposition with each other? To say this is not to revert to a definition of culture as a closed and static field. Transcultural overlap, class and social differences, discourse and counterdiscourse—all can be accounted for by looking at the process of the cultural imaginary in this way.

Cultural Personas and Social Stratification

If personas have this kind of representational function, then, as noted, it makes perfect sense that they would be created over time and represent values and understandings associated with social divisions or different social segments—whether class, subculture, or other. It also makes sense that at least some of the personas originating with, or popular among, subaltern or subordinate strata would represent a conglomeration of contesting meanings vis-à-vis the dominant social groups. There are clear elements of this in the narcotrafficker persona, and these elements are quite similar to aspects of certain personas that I have encountered as characteristic of high-poverty urban settings, for example, the dealer or hustler persona.

With the "urban dealer" persona, the emphasis again is on performance, on establishing a reputation and carrying out a daily performance that validates the performer as a dealer and deserving of a reputation as one who makes things happen. The reputation must include a willingness to be ruthless when necessary (e.g., when territory or reputation is challenged or when double-crossed), a show of wealth as a demonstration of efficacy and ability (and as a not-so-subtle rejection of the dominant society's rules for how properly to achieve success), and, in the most enduring examples, at least the pretense of attachment to community (in the form of services, help, and money provided to community members). Maintaining this kind of reputation is a richly coded task. I used to hear, for example, that the way to hold a gun during a shooting was horizontally, with arm extended out to the side as opposed to in front. This was a stylized way of demonstrating power and insouciance vis-à-vis the victim.

While the details are different, this is very close to some of the basic elements of the narcotrafficker persona. Moreover, there is a striking similarity in the way that both personas (narcotrafficker and dealer), as symbols, appear simultaneously to contest and accept dominant group meanings with respect to the criteria for establishing oneself as a "significant" or admired person. Like Warner's (1959) parable of the disfavored but socially mobile outsider Biggy Muldoon, there is both a tendency to want in via demonstrations of the material trappings of success and a rejection of the dominant rules for how to get there, the accepted "cultural performance of success." Since having status or being notable is such a symbolically laden task, an individual who rejects participation in that performance may be precluded from ever really being there. (Yet, on the other hand, such a person may end up as the progenitor of a new model of acceptable cultural performance for "success" or status, or even gender role.) This, in fact, is one of the subtle ways in which racism and other forms of discrimination work even when the overt or de jure constraints are gone. Moreover, if one does attempt the cultural performance along with the material performance, the dilemma so often lies in the consequent rejection of oneself, and therefore one's original reference group—as described in the classic work by Whyte (1993) with respect to Chick Morelli, the former "corner boy" who became a success in the mainstream world. Thus one of the comments I heard repeatedly during this research about Chalino Sánchez, who was both narcocorrido singer and a (reputed) narcotrafficker himself, and who made a substantial amount of money from his music, was that he "valued his people" over the money and status he gained, and that he "never left his people."

A third, and important, parallel (noted earlier) is in the way that death seems to *complete* the persona, such that death is not the ending, but the "launching" of an individual into a timeless existence as an iteration of the persona whose life will float in the popular imaginary: reputation cemented and memorialized forever, free from the barriers that prevented attainment of full status in this world. As noted, there are cultural roots in Mexico for this with respect to the narcotrafficker persona, but since this is a characteristic of personas that exist in other settings, it is not just a cultural idiosyncrasy. Something else is involved. It is possible that, in a situation of poverty where options for being a "significant" person are limited or perceived as limited (at least in this world), a notable death in fact becomes one way of living, one way of having made a dent in the cosmos, so to speak. This sentiment may exist across cultures in situations of social stratification and poverty, and may be embodied in culturally specific ways through the invention of personas such as have been described here. In this society, at least, poverty—among other things—is facelessness; yet people yearn to be known, to have had an existence that left at least some trace.[5] Moreover, it is not a great leap to say that, in a global context of stratification by nation-state, by center-periphery, by West/non-West, or other such divisions, these general sentiments are kin to the ethic of martyrdom, which is so common among those who are called terrorists.

Recall Woody Guthrie's description of the outlaw and his explanation of why outlaws draw the kind of popular support they do. With the narcotrafficker persona, however, there is less clarity with respect to which are represented as dominant or subordinate groups. Moreover, the element of racial polarization that is part of the urban U.S. dealer persona is not so clearly part of the narcotrafficker persona. In El Paso/Juárez, and other locations on the border, socioeconomic disparities cannot always be essentialized a priori as coterminous with racial or ethnic categories, since populations on both sides of the border are predominantly Mexican in ethnic origin (see Martínez 1988, 1994), and the dominant subgroups (in socioeconomic terms) include either (1) Anglo, Mexican, and other foreign nationals who own or manage maquilas and their related businesses; or (2) "druglords." In Juárez, I saw a number of walled neighborhoods and compounds where the elite or top families live. These are largely Mexican families. And there are narcocorrido lyrics that focus on the Mexican police just as there are those that focus on the U.S. Border Patrol and the INS. In a way, the lack of clarity allows for more exploitation of the persona, because the ambiguity can be glossed over or presented in ways that are more suggestive than clear.

Linking Transcendent Cultural Personas to Individual Action

The issue of linkage between media-disseminated images or personas and individual action (or practice) is complex, though it is an issue that has flooded public discourse in the United States once again, following the recent string of school shootings. We can say that, as for other expressive genres, corridos and narcocorridos are part of a package that includes what some call "behavior," because behavior and its representation are hard to separate. Yet this is where "behavior" can, or should, be considered as an element of the semiotics of self, in the manner that Bourdieu (1977) has linked presentation of the body and ideology. In this light, then, do narco-corridos, or any such widely disseminated media representations, influence action? As noted earlier, no one in any interview directly attributed any specific actions or activities that they were or had been involved in, or specific actions of others, to narcocorridos per se. But if narcocorridos present an image of the embodied persona, then they provide cultural material—an objectified self (or object for mimesis) from which an individual can make himself or herself an instantiation of the values represented in the persona, in a Bakhtinian, dialogic sense. Being an instantiation means clothes, a "bodily hexis," an attitude toward death and risk, a preoccupation with projecting power and importance, and other ways in which the persona is articulated with daily life: bodyguards, jewelry, a shiny black Dodge Ram truck, hat, belt, shirt, boots, the appearance (or the reality) of having business to conduct at almost any time.

The interview and observation data also suggest that narcocorridos, because they are now mass-media products, also celebretize an arena of behavior, by the very act of foregrounding it in a media form that has the role of, and is expected to, celebretize arenas of behavior. Celebretizing in this way does not necessarily mean that all the actions foregrounded are perceived as "good," only that they are deemed important, noteworthy, and thus have status. Moreover, because in this case the media form is also the corrido form, the celebretization takes on, to some listeners, a vague but culturally shaped sense of social critique that resonates with other factors existing in their lives and thus validates the celebretized behavior in a broader social/cultural context, because corridos are a cultural form already marked for that interpretation.

Thus if the interview responses and observations are valid, they certainly suggest that narcotrafficker behavior, the presentation of self-as-narcotrafficker, has a kind of socially grounded celebrity associated with it. And as Goffman (1959) has noted, this kind of self-presentation is an ongoing game of sorts, which not only requires appearing in character, but may also require validation of a different kind. That is, if one is presenting as a "dangerous" or "power-ful" character, sooner or later one may face a situation in which commensurate action is called for to maintain the presentation as valid. This is one kind of occasion where the persona-as-celebrity and what is called "risk behavior" (drug sales, violence) meet.

At the same time, I would argue that narcocorridos—and other music or media of the same type in other cultural situations—do not have a determining effect on behavior, though they can have a reinforcing and shaping effect. Media such as this provide a culturally resonant shape and coherence for certain patterns of action that are already under way to one degree or another (or if not already under way, highly imminent) for other, more proximate, reasons. These reasons include personal circumstances (family difficulties, family health problems, neglect, substance abuse, etc.) that are often a product of the larger structural condition of poverty and coexisting—and glaring—income and power differences that are so concentrated in an urban setting. The music and the media image the persona helps to shape a symbolic structure for individual action (or behavior), such that the actions can be integrated into a coherent sense of self. Put another way, the media forms provide a "packaged" cultural trajectory to follow, with all that entails in terms of meanings, values, norms, and a social stance that is contained within the packed media symbol. The persona and actions associated with it are a sign in a symbolically structured world. As such, the media representation may make these patterns of action more difficult to change, because the actions are now ensconced in a self-image in such a way that outside attempts to change them will be perceived as changing the self, and may thus be resisted.

Is this like saying the narcotrafficker persona is a social model (in the manner of Bandura 1986)? Not exactly. First, the connection between a mythologized persona such as the narcotrafficker and specific action is rarely a direct one in the sense of "because I saw/heard a narcotrafficker do x, I went and did x." Neither is it that a narcotrafficker becomes an example in a process of observational learning, where he or she models behavior for others, who then learn the behaviors and increase their sense of efficacy—although this is closer to the mark. It is, I would argue, a step or more removed, yet in a very important way. The narcotrafficker becomes a symbol, a persona who represents a whole aggregation of values and meanings. As such, one does more than just model behavior after the persona; one seeks to construct one's self, one's being, as an iteration of the persona in order to express the same relationship to the larger world that the persona does.

Let us assume, without trying to be overly glib, that on the U.S.-Mexico border, the narcotrafficker persona draws some part of its meaning from (1) conditions of poverty set against the domination (perceived and real, in different measures) of global industry (via the maquilas), the United States, and the still-salient class and race structure in Mexico; (2) the long tradition of border conflict between the United States and Mexico, and the underlying antagonism that flows from the conflict;[6] (3) a Mexican tradition of individuals as centers of power and agency—the tradition of *personalismo* (Suchlicki 1996); and (4) long-held images of a northern Mexican man, clever, brave, and tough. The narcotrafficker then represents a certain, culturally shaped, individual route to power for those who feel powerless, a challenge to the customary "rules" for how one achieves status and influence, and a route to status for those usually shut out (as outlined earlier). Thus it is not just the modeling effect which is key. In constructing oneself as an iteration of the narcotrafficker persona, one takes on the stance that this persona represents. Particular behaviors, including violence and drug use, are not simply mechanical imitations of a model, but are pursued to the extent that they are part of the expression of that stance.

In the context of the border, this kind of representation is powerful. Moreover, I would argue, that same, or similar representations are just as salient in other situations of poverty, disaffection, and alienation—whether that is in the inner city, a rural area, or somewhere else. Fleisher (1998) has documented, for example, how youth gang leaders are mythologized, again, not just as models, but as representations of a stance. Bourgois (1989, 1996) has noted the connection between crack selling and respect in New York City. Anderson (1992) has described a young man's involvement in drugs as a redress of the humiliation experienced in the mainstream world. In my own experience, I have encountered a number of examples (see Edberg 1998, and Chapter 1 in this book).

Consequently, actions that are often spoken of as "risk behaviors" need to be viewed as more than behaviors: they are also expressions. This is, of course, not the only factor involved, and it may be more or less important in different cases. But the discourse of "behavior" tends to push aside these considerations in establishing causality and in developing social and health prevention and intervention modalities. As discussed below, a prevention/intervention approach that views behavior also as expression, I would argue, must address that which is being expressed through specific behaviors and seek to resolve or change what lies behind the expressive stance, or to find other ways through which it can be channeled.

The Persistence and Reinvention of Personas as Cultural Representations

The issue of the persona as a mode for transmitting cultural representations "out into the cosmos" addresses Sperber's (1996) concerns with the question of how only a selection of public representations remain over time and become cultural. Framing the discussion using an epidemiological model, Sperber asks (pp. 57, 58), "Why are some representations 'catching,' while others are not?" Or, "Why are we susceptible to some representations more than others?" While one does not have to agree with all of Sperber's answers to these questions—he is, by his own admission, a materialist in the sense that he looks toward biosocial processes as determining—some of his conclusions are interesting and relevant to this discussion.

If, for example, we retain representations that are evocative and relevant, then the notion of persona makes some sense. Evocative representations, says Sperber (1996, p. 73), are those which "on the one hand, are closely related to the subject's other mental representations, and, on the other hand, can never be given a final interpretation." In other words, they are open-ended. And they are symbolic, but grounded. A persona is by nature an instance of this kind of "fuzzy logic." It can and does appear in incomplete forms, as masked or transformed, or only by reference in absentia, or in opposition. Anyone, for example, who has worked with lawyers, particularly lawyers in large litigation firms, will recognize a type that could be called the "legal cowboy." These are lawyers who are on the road quite a bit and who place a high value on their reputation (which may include being known as a hard drinker, or having a sharp wit, or showing no quarter in court), because court battles are viewed as showdowns between opposing lawyers, much like the classic archetype of the cowboy or gunslinger. I would argue that here a cultural persona is recycled and surfaces in a particular occupation as a "type," as a mode of action and self-presentation, which represents a cluster of values and meanings that are expressed through a particular form of conflict that is many steps removed from the arena of conflict characteristic of the persona in its original, or "pure," form (though no such persona will be without historical antecedents). This legal type is a reverberation of a powerful American cultural persona, but this time given definition within the world of the legal profession. In other arenas, it may surface as the "Marlboro man," or as a series of Clint Eastwood film characters.

But personas like the narcotrafficker persona, while open-ended, are so only to an extent. They are, I will speculate broadly, relevant for the subordinate because their basic meaning is referential or deictic (Levinson 1983) with respect to place in a social hierarchy. They are by nature a comment of some sort on that hierarchy. Interestingly enough, because they have that reference, those who are not in subordinate positions take that referential meaning out of context and tend to appropriate such symbols as indicative of rebellion. This is clear in the way music-related personas from African American street culture have been appropriated, whether from rock-and-roll or hip-hop. It is also true with the narcotrafficker persona, which has an attraction even among the youth from wealthy families in Mexico, where, as noted earlier, it has a kind of hip cachet that seems clearly tied to its meaning as beyond, or in conflict with, the general system of social rules.

In addition, cultural personas are dialogic in the Bakhtinian sense, because they function in a manner like "ventriloquation" (Bakhtin 1981; see also discussion in Wertsch 1991), only in this case not at the utterance level, but at the person or self level. That is, they are symbolic units in a social language (discourse) of self, such that individuals "populate" the symbols and make them their own. By doing so, though, they are always engaging with the ongoing, historical discourse to produce a self expressed, and thus shaped, through another. This is also something like the process of mimesis described by Taussig (1993, p. xiii): the mimetic faculty that "culture uses to create second nature, the faculty to copy, imitate, make models, explore difference, yield into and become Other."

In the case of the narcotrafficker persona, is its "resonance" primarily situated in Mexican cultural roots? I would argue that its initial shape is "Mexican"—or more specifically, northern Mexican—but its essence, as described, is transcultural. Its transcultural resonance, as I have argued, comes in part from shared situations of social stratification (now entwined with shared constructions of what these situations are and mean), but is also the result of the mass media's blending and appropriation of a mix of representations and the broad dissemination of personas or archetypes beyond their geospatial roots.

A more harshly critical version of this thesis has been articulated by Mexican essayist and social critic Carlos Monsiváis. He has argued that the narcotrafficker persona as represented in narcocorridos and the proliferation of narcofilms owes a great deal to cultural imperialism from the characters in American westerns, the John Wayne and Clint Eastwood archetypes. Says Monsiváis (from Thelen 1999): "The narcos tried to be norteños in a sense new in Mexico, one that didn't exist before the 1960s, norteños like John Wayne or the Marlboro Man or Clint Eastwood, or a Vietnam veteran turned FBI man. . . . It may not be conscious, but the narcos' walk, their outfits, their idea of a he-man, the obsession with guns—all come from American western movies. John Wayne and his gun. And the narco is a he-man with a lot of guns." This may, however, be overstating the case. After all, as we have seen, gun-slinging corrido heroes have been around since well before John Wayne, though some influence is highly probable.

To sum up, then, this study argues for a conception of the cultural persona as a representational form that encapsulates and provides for perpetuation, interaction, opposition, change, and, generally, fluidity, of cultural understandings, values, beliefs, and practices— and that links understandings, values, and beliefs with practices, by showing them in action. Where the range of understandings, values, beliefs, and linked practices is represented through a "fuzzy set" of personas, it could be said that

- widely disseminated cultural understandings, values, beliefs;
- elite/dominant understandings, values, beliefs;
- subaltern understandings, values, beliefs;
- transcultural understandings, values, beliefs;
- subgroup understandings, values, beliefs;

. . . are incorporated into (or contested in) a set of cultural personas which are perpetuated and evolve over time (as "culture"), through

- media (including advertising), narratives, literature, mythologies, commonsense sayings, and so on, which deploy the personas in various combinations, oppositions, and "plots," thus maintaining a loose but ongoing presence of a "cultural field" populated by personas;
- individual practice—appropriation and reiteration of the persona in different (individual) contexts;
- transcultural importation and blending through media and personal interaction; and
- the introduction of new personas—internally, out of changing historical circumstances, or transculturally, through direct and mediated interaction.

Clearly, it has to be said that the various mass media accelerate the process because of their reach, their daily engagement with individuals, and their propensity to utilize cultural personas as commodities, precisely because they carry such a symbolic load. Figure 2 depicts this process and how it is perpetuated.

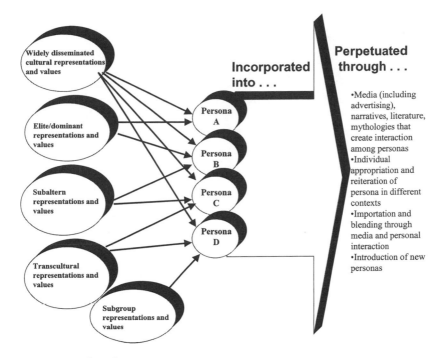

Figure 2. Cultural Personas

Narcocorridos versus Classic Corridos

Finally, an important research question concerned the relationship between narcocorridos and classic, or traditional, corridos. It is important to note that both Paredes (1958) and Mendoza (1944) are harshly critical of corridos written after the 1930s, arguing that they lost their "genuineness" or were cheapened by their dissemination in the emerging mass media. Paredes (1993, p. 139, quoted in Nicolopulos 1997, pp. 116–117), for example, denigrates these emerging corridos in the following critique:

After 1930, when Mexico's Tin Pan Alley took over the corrido, its decay was inevitable. At first radio and the movies employed folksingers and composers, and Mexican popular music had a brief golden age. But soon the demand for more and more new songs wore the folk material thin. A type of song developed that is to the true corrido what American hillbilly music is to the British folk ballad. Perhaps the ultimate was reached when Mexico's double-barreled answer to Gene Autry and Frank

Sinatra, the late Pedro Infante, groaned a pseudo-corrido into a microphone while a bevy of Mexican bobby-soxers squealed in ecstasy.

No doubt Paredes would have had a field day attending a contemporary narcocorrido concert or hearing narcocorridos blasting on a car radio. However, it is likely true that there have always been corridos that are more the epic and serious coexisting with a broad range of other corridos—perhaps less "pure" in form and sentiment. And yet the form and meaning of the corrido continues through time, to be, in a sense, picked up as history and circumstances dictate. Even as narcocorridos were beginning to emerge in the 1970s, people involved in the Chicano movement around the same time sang corridos about César Chávez, about immigration, about protest marches or events, and about other related themes, for inspiration.

Based on the research results, my conclusion is that narcocorridos are in some ways a transformation of the "classic" corrido form, occasioned by their inclusion in the arena of modern mass media. At the same time, they retain the social footing, to some extent, of classic corridos; they would not have the popularity they do if they did not resonate with existing cultural themes together with modern realities. The old corridos were about heroes, about vengeance, about the loneliness and vicissitudes of the immigration experience, about injustice, and about love lost. They were sung by people for people, interpreted differently along the way within the general understanding of the corrido community. They were longer, more imbued with references to mothers and friends and community— this is true even for the smuggler corridos of the Prohibition era.

Narcocorridos, in my view, draw from this tradition, but in doing so are both corridos and cynical simulacra of corridos. They are popular, yes, and the narcotraffickers they sing about are often popular. And, as noted in the review of data, people do submit "homegrown" corrido lyrics to bands that perform, including big-name bands, thereby retaining a certain community quality in the genre. Yet narcocorridos are popular in part because they have entered the world of mass-media image making, where the essence of the old corrido is diluted by transforming it into a mere vehicle for selling, where the featured characters (narcotraffickers) are constructed to appeal to popular sentiments on the one hand, but to create a fantastic and compelling image on the other, because images are a draw. Adding to the complexity, a significant number of narcocorridos do not come from the "people," but from narcotraffickers themselves, or from those who are in the business of selling popular music. Because the image of the social bandit, the Pancho Villa, is so powerfully embedded in northern Mexican tradition, it becomes possible to construct narcotraffickers, in some fashion, in their image. And it pays. Many narcocorridos come into existence because a narcotrafficker contacts someone who writes or sings corridos and requests—as a paid service—that they write a narcocorrido about them.

Are narcocorridos some form of counterdiscourse, some form of political statement driven by social conditions as refracted through a cultural lens, in the manner argued by Paredes for classic corridos? Yes and no. They are, as I have shown, on the one hand, mere simulacra—hollowed-out versions of corridos for the purpose of making money by working through a "thick" cultural form. In this sense, they are nothing like the classic corridos. Once again, however, we return to a key point. Narcocorridos could not exert the popular pull that they do unless they touched on sentiments that are widespread, and touched these sentiments via a cultural form that is marked for such sentiments. It is here that, in my view, the narcocorridos do draw from, and intermingle with, commonly shared understandings about oppositions of social position: Mexicans versus Anglos, Mexico versus the United States, Mexicans of a rural or poor background versus Mexicans of elite background, and, in general, northern/border Mexican peoples versus the central Mexican government and those who represent them (police, government officials, etc). These are representations based on what I will call the "stratified other." In this sense, these data support the epidemiological model offered by Sperber (1996) to explain why some representations become enduring, shared representations—and thus "cultural"—while others do not.

Applied Implications

Although the research described in this book is not applied research per se, there are implications for applied work. Some of these are as follows.

Working with the Persona

First, recall that those working in or through public health, social service, and justice agencies generally operate within a behavioral science model, in which programs are targeted to behaviors (as either interventions or prevention). Let us assume that personas

such as the narcotrafficker persona in the narcocorridos serve a socially, culturally grounded, organizing function; that is, they provide coherence, significance, and meaning to a pattern of behavior such that it can now be integrated as an inherent part of being
(or "acting as if") that persona—a persona that will be understood
as such by at least some set of people with whom one interacts. If
true, then the "behaviors" associated with the persona cannot be
viewed as individual behaviors in the way that prevention science
tends to do. This is even more so in the case of a persona that draws
from deep historical (or mythological) antecedents: a cultural persona. Attempts to change specific behaviors may well be rejected
because these will be viewed as a threat to the integrity of one's
adopted persona (one's personal structure of coherence, as it were).

The more effective approach in this kind of situation is thus not
to challenge the persona and what it represents, but to find out what
is represented, work with it, and (through media interventions, targeted peer "modeling," or other interventions) seek to include more
"positive" behaviors within the ambit of the persona, so that someone could engage in the positive behaviors while still maintaining
himself or herself in the role of that persona.

Reevaluating the Discourse of Risk

If the role and meaning of the social bandit, or outlaw, persona is
valid as set forth in this book, then it is necessary to reevaluate the
discourse of risk behavior. Risk is a subjective concept, and (as described) risk of death or other misfortune is an inherent, ontological element of a persona such as the narcotrafficker as represented
in narcocorridos. Thinking in terms of risk behavior is therefore
relevant only within the public health agency or provider sphere,
but largely irrelevant to many of those who are the intended subjects and beneficiaries of public health programs. This is particularly true where someone's behavior is organized around a coherent
persona or symbolic structure as described here, and particularly
when the persona has important cultural roots as well as roots in
a specific socioeconomic context of poverty, racism, or alienation.
As noted above, behavior specificity may simply not be the way
such intended subjects think about what they do. Further, programs
or media messages that follow a linear "logic model" or behavior
path approach may ultimately be less effective than programs that
link clusters of behaviors with the meanings attributed by those involved to those behavior clusters, then focus on "de-linking" behaviors from the cluster, or, as noted, replacing or expanding behav-

ior choices within the cluster—in combination with broader efforts that, over the long term, address the complex of social or economic factors that lend meaning to and support the risk behaviors.

Finally, it just may be that the real risk for people in a high-poverty existence may be, as discussed previously, to have been unseen, unknown, without power or efficacy, with no "cosmic dent" to their credit. If this is true, behaviors characteristic of the narcotrafficker image are a form of prevention in themselves. They are engaged in prevention; it is just prevention of something very different from what is foregrounded by the public health community, a kind of existential-level prevention.

Multiple Interpretations of Media Representations

It is also very important to note that, for prevention messages—or in assessing the impact of "negative" media messages—such messages or representations have multiple interpretations: by context, by age, by situation and the co-presence of peers, and other factors. To understand how a media representation will be interpreted, better information is needed on these multiple interpretations. It is erroneous to overstate or rest a case on one type of interpretation, yet that is the tendency when an event—like the Columbine High School shootings—creates an urgent public need for explanation.

Nonmainstream Media Channels

Based on the case of narcocorridos—which may be representative of other media—any assessment of the effectiveness of health-related prevention messages must also give adequate attention to the range of nonmainstream channels through which messages are heard. Media and music such as narcocorridos are typically not disseminated primarily through mainstream media channels; if they are, they are interpreted differently in those settings. There is a wide range of channels through which listeners hear and see narcotrafficker images and narcocorridos, including word of mouth, street distribution of tapes and CDs, underground film, cantina jukeboxes, and social gatherings.

Finally, this brief study has made abundantly clear the extent to which cultural images cross political boundaries via contemporary mass media and shape or are shaped by the market forces propelling the directionality of these images. Media products are targeted, and targeted to potential audiences based on various calculations of potential receptivity, whether these are demographic or other factors. In the Hispanic world, narcocorridos are no longer just "Mexican" or "Mexican border" in terms of their reach and the "community" within which they have meaning. A narcocorrido website is based in Argentina. Major music groups that play narcocorridos appear on Univisión (a Hispanic cable television network), which is syndicated across the United States. And, only a few days ago, I stopped to eat in a Salvadoran restaurant in the Washington, D.C., area, and the first sound I heard coming through the door was a narcocorrido from the jukebox.

CHALINO SANCHEZ

Con La Banda Santa Cruz
CORRIDOS VILLISTAS

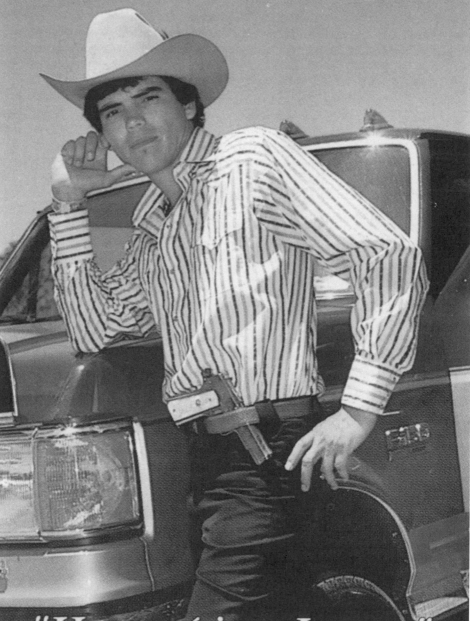

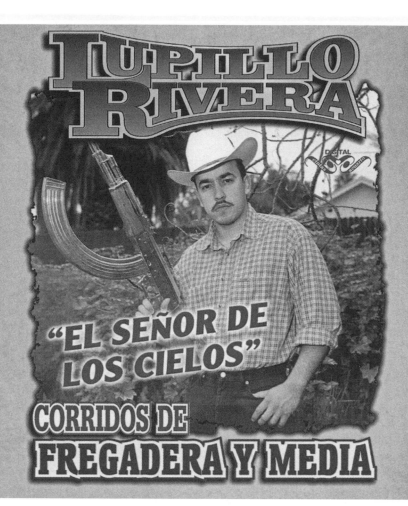

LUPILLO RIVERA

DIGITAL

"EL SEÑOR DE LOS CIELOS"

CORRIDOS DE FREGADERA Y MEDIA

Appendix 1. Research Methodology and Sample Interview Guides

Summary of Research Methods

The study design was, of necessity, a case study (see Bernard 1988). Because it was exploratory in nature and funded only as a pilot, an experimental or quasi-experimental design was not feasible, or desirable, at this stage. There was no "testing" of any sort of intervention or specific hypotheses, but we attempted to gain some preliminary insight regarding a set of research questions. Generally, the research followed an ethnographic process, seeking to build data inductively around a general set of questions and to utilize the following broad steps:

A. An initial list of contacts/key informants and a process for gaining entry into the study community and becoming familiar with the general situation with respect to social circumstances (community characteristics, employment and poverty, housing) and attitudes (toward drug use, narco-trafficking, U.S.-Mexico issues, etc.);

B. Progressively more specific, iterative interviewing, broadening the contact network, and conducting participant-observation to assess knowledge gained through interviews and situate that knowledge in context, "in its natural setting";

C. Informal interviews (with no set agenda and used to identify directions or themes to pursue), semistructured interviews (with an agenda of topics or questions, open-ended, narrative response format), and focus groups (group discussion with an agenda) (see below for examples of interview guides used);

D. Tape-recording of interviews where feasible; otherwise

recording responses and observations on specific forms or as field notes; and

E. Analysis of interview and observation data for commonalities and themes vis-à-vis research questions.

A number of individuals and groups (noted in the Acknowledgments) offered significant assistance in data collection and interpretation. Again, however, I express my deep gratitude to all of them for their for their assistance, interest, and insights.

Sample

In the initial plan, the primary data collection sample was to be structured as a *quota sample* (as defined in Bernard 1988), with quota criteria and proportions determined following initial research activities in which the composition of the narcocorrido listener population was to be clarified. (The sample was to include individuals who were producers as well as consumers of the narcocorridos.) In fact, the sample was more of a *convenience sample*, though guided by quota criteria. The realities of fieldwork with limited resources simply precluded a rigorous attempt to recruit for interviews by quota. The attempt was made to do so, but it was conditioned by the availability of respondents at any given time, and by the naturally imprecise process of setting up and conducting interviews through individuals and organizations who work in the community. During the study period, the following interviews and observations were conducted:

- Interviews with seventeen youth in Juárez (mostly male), and ten in El Paso (five male, five female), age ranges about twelve to early twenties. In addition, two focus groups: one in a Chicano studies class (fifteen students) at UTEP; one in a social work class at the Universidad Autónoma de Ciudad Juárez (about eight students). Youth interviews included persons interviewed in various Juárez colonias, the juvenile jail, and an El Paso gang prevention program;
- Interviews with about twenty-eight adults on both sides of the border, including four individuals from radio stations in Juárez that play norteño music (including corridos), two members of a popular border-area norteño music group in Douglas, Arizona, two adults involved with an alcohol and substance use program in El Paso, a support group (of five men) in El Paso who were recently released from jail or

prison, three officials at the Juárez prison, three inmates, three individuals who worked at maquilas (one of whom had left to start his own business), a man who was a member of the Rio Grande River Commission, staff at a public health program called Compañeros (Juárez), and several instructors at UTEP (in Chicano studies);

- In Los Angeles, interviews with two individuals from the marketing department at a major record company's Latino music subsidiary (sponsor of major narcocorrido performers Los Tucanes de Tijuana) and three individuals at a smaller recording studio. (In addition to recording, the studio produced and distributed tapes and CDs.) A site visit was conducted to the latter operation (in Long Beach, California);
- Observation of a major narcocorrido performance (by Los Tigres del Norte); of local narcocorrido and norteño music performances at cantinas, at the Juárez city jail, and at "narcobars," in both Juárez and El Paso; of living conditions in several of the colonias in Juárez (e.g., Bella Vista, Alta Vista, Revolución); of the central prison and youth prison in Juárez; and of various aspects of daily life in El Paso and Juárez generally (e.g., a Kermess, or community festival, in El Paso, markets, cantinas, a youth substance abuse prevention program, community rally, and at-home situations in Juárez); and
- Many informal conversations on the street in Juárez.

Protocols used in the interviews (semistructured interview guides) are included in this Appendix. Generally, interviews were conducted in the field and were simultaneous with participant-observation.

Research Questions and Methods Used

Specific research questions and subquestions and the methods used to investigate them are as follows:

QUESTION ONE: What kind of narcotrafficker archetype or persona is represented in the narcocorridos, and how is this representation achieved? What relation does it have to the "hero image" of traditional corridos?

This question was investigated through

A. preliminary narrative analysis of the narcocorridos.
   To gain an initial understanding of the narcocorrido

content, the persona(s) they contain, and the manner of representation, a selection of narcocorridos was transcribed and translated for narrative analysis, to assess the following:

- The general form and character of narcocorridos compared with those of "classic" corridos as an initial means of assessing whether or not the narcotraffickers are represented as heroes in the manner of the heroes of classic corridos. "Form" most often refers to narrative structure (e.g., repetitive elements, bracketing, voice), metaphor, and other linguistic aspects (Riessman 1993; McDowell 1981; Sapir and Crocker 1977). For example, both traditional corridos and narco-corridos use the boast and the insult as predominant speech acts (McDowell 1981), and both use metaphors derived from the "ballad community"[1] of which the music is a part. Narcocorridos, like much Mexican and Spanish slang about socially sensitive topics, also appear to make liberal use of double entendre. In narcocorridos, many references and meanings are also coded—data collection and analysis sought to identify these.
- Semantic content—common descriptive characteristics of the narcotrafficker persona featured in these songs and the portrayal of the narcotrafficker's exploits: What kinds of exploits are foregrounded? How are these exploits represented: as triumphs? justice done? revenge? demonstrations of power? Against what background are the exploits presented as having meaning? What is the persona like: cruel? sympathetic? dashing? violent? Are there any references to the persona *as a man?* How do these characterizations compare with the traditional corrido hero? Other common thematic elements will be assessed: glory? loneliness? victimization at the hands of Anglo or Mexican police? References to the social or economic situation on the border? How do these other common themes compare to those that might be found in the traditional corrido? General approaches to narrative construction of self were consulted (e.g., Riessman 1993; Linde 1989; Hankiss 1981).

B. interviews and participant observation
As the companion to a narrative analysis of the narco-corridos, I collected data relevant to this question from informal, semistructured, and focus group interviews conducted with both producers (individuals at radio

stations, music outlets, studios, musicians themselves) and the consumer (listener) sample. These interviews included questions on respondent understandings of themes, content, presentation of the narcotrafficker image, multiple meanings, and contexts for listening. During some interviews, questions were asked after playing tapes of one or more narcocorridos. Some data on the narcocorrido persona came from participant-observation as well, particularly while observing live performances.

QUESTION TWO: What social factors are related to themes common in narcocorridos and to the ways in which the narcocorridos are interpreted? What do narcocorridos "say" about these kinds of themes? Given the traditional social role of corridos, these were logical questions to ask about narcocorridos.

This question was investigated through

A. interviews with individuals at radio stations, music outlets, studios, and musicians (producers): these focused on identifying the listening audience, social factors relevant to the listening audience, and what producers saw as the meaning or appeal of the music;

B. interviews with a sample of narcocorrido listeners (consumers): focusing on how listeners "represent the representations" in the narcocorridos, and what factors are related to their interpretation. Questions include

- extent and circumstances of listening;
- how narcocorridos are generally interpreted and viewed (and by whom);
- understandings of violence and drug use as portrayed in narcocorridos;
- identity group(s) of reference for listeners (and is there an us-them "othering" process related to the identity groups?);
- social, economic, and cultural factors related to interpretation—such as employment and economic circumstances, perceptions of social differentiation, admired persons, attributes of status in the community, future expectations; and
- conceptions of the narcotrafficker in view of such factors.

C. Participant-observation: collected data and observations on when narcocorridos are played, by whom, in what context, and the living conditions and socioeconomic status of those among whom they are popular. These observations were assessed in comparison with what interview respondents said concerning the same themes.

QUESTION THREE: How does the technology of modern mass-media production impact upon the way in which the narcocorrido representations are constructed, disseminated, and to whom they are disseminated? Investigated primarily through interviews along with some observation among a small sample of producers; at radio stations, music outlets, studios, and musicians themselves. Questions included the following:

A. How are narcocorridos produced—who writes them, who sings them, who backs them (financially), who records them, etc.?
B. Who distributes them? Where are they distributed?
C. How and when are they played?
D. What is/are the marketing concept(s) employed? What demand are they "playing to"? What is the role of violence and other aspects of the narcotrafficker image in their "marketability"?

QUESTION FOUR: How is the narcotrafficker persona, as portrayed in the corridos, connected to daily practice (behavior) among listeners? This question was investigated through

A. interviews (with narcocorrido listeners and consumers): questions on expressed desire to emulate narcotraffickers, as heroes of the narcocorridos; instances or patterns of actual emulation; results of emulation/reactions to emulation;
B. Participant-observation: participant-observation occurred simultaneously with interviews described above. Generally, participant-observation included time spent among the listener sample in El Paso and Juárez in a range of activities, including norteño and narcocorrido performances, community events, day-to-day activities, in cantinas and bars, and (with Compañeros staff in Juárez, Back on Track staff in El Paso) on outreach and community prevention activities. One goal of the participant-observation was to assess any day-to-day connections between the narcocorrido persona and day-to-day behavior. For attendance at narcocorrido performances, the focus was on assessing the

narcocorridos as *event,* focusing on performer and audience actions and expressions. Here the "data elements" were to include performance characteristics; kinesics and proxemics (and clothing) associated with the "bodily hexis" of the narcocorrido persona (for performers and audience members); the presence of audience expressive elements common within the "expressive ecology" of the border corrido and related music forms (McDowell 1981); and speech styles and linguistic elements—understanding (e.g., from Hymes 1974) that these elements encode a social semiotic.

Data Analysis and Reporting

Field notes, qualitative data collected in unstructured and semi-structured interviews, and other narrative and textual data were recorded on tape where feasible, or recorded on forms or in field notes. Where necessary, they were translated from Spanish. Analysis proceeded as follows:

A. Coding and analyzing text: transcribed and/or written text data were reviewed and analyzed for common themes in the areas of research interest. The common themes were assessed thoroughly in terms of content expressed and in terms of the characteristics of individuals who were the sources of the text data;

B. Narrative descriptions: analysis also consisted of event and activity descriptions, culled from field notes, which contain descriptions of participants, flow of events, nature of event/activity, and the content of the event/activity.

Confidentiality

Confidentiality was maintained throughout the research process. No data were reported with individual identifiers; all qualitative data are reported using pseudonyms or in the aggregate, as trends or patterns.

Questionnaire on Narcocorridos

1. Do you ever listen to corridos? YES__ NO__

IF YOU ANSWERED YES, PLEASE ANSWER THE FOLLOWING QUESTIONS:

2. Where do you usually hear them (on the radio? on tapes or CDs? other places?)?

3. Can you name some of the groups you know that play corridos?

4. Do you like the corridos you have heard? YES__ NO__

IF YOU ANSWERED YES:

A. What do you like most about them?
__ The music
__ The words—the stories or events that happen in the song
__ The person or persons featured in the song
__ Other: _____

5. Are any of the corridos you have heard about people (*traficantes*) who bring drugs across the border (to be sold in the U.S.)?
YES__ NO__

IF YOU ANSWERED YES:

A. What do you think about these people (traficantes)? Are they people to admire? Not to admire? Why?

B. What do the corridos say about them (traficantes)?

6. Name three things that you think make a person important or admirable:

One: _____
Two: _____
Three: _____

Do the persons sung about in the corridos have any of these characteristics? YES__ NO__

IF YOU ANSWERED YES:

Which ones? [CHECK ALL THAT APPLY]

One__
Two__
Three__

Interview Questions for Narcocorrido Producers

1. What musical groups do you work with that play corridos (e.g., Los Tucanes, etc.)? Where are they generally from?

2. Who is the listening audience? (Demographics) From both U.S. and Mexico? Or primarily Mexico?

3. What stories do these new corridos tell? What and who are they about? Are they like/not like traditional corridos in the sense of recounting the exploits of heroes?

IF YES:

What makes the characters in these corridos heroes? [Narcocorridos]

4. Do the corridos contain any "messages," or any content about the social situation? Examples?

5. What is their major appeal? Does it differ by listening audience segment?

6. How do you usually market them and where? How do you address the issue of narcocorridos being banned from some media outlets (e.g., radio)?

7. Is there anything else that would help me understand their appeal?

Questionnaire on Corridos (for use at concert/event)

TO RESPONDENT: We are doing a short survey to learn about popular corridos and corrido bands, and to find out more about what makes them popular. It will only take a few minutes of your time.

1. Is this the first time you have seen [insert band name]?
YES__ NO__

2. Where do you usually hear [insert band name]? On the radio? on tapes or CDs? other places?

3. Are there other groups you know that play corridos like [insert band name]?

IF YES:

Can you name some of these groups?

4. Who would you say usually listens to corridos (like the kind played by [insert band name])? Younger people? Older people? Men? Women?

5. What do you like most about these corridos?

__ The music
__ The words—the stories or events that happen in the song
__ The person or persons featured in the song
__ Other: _____

6. Which corridos, by [insert band name] or another group, are your favorites? PLEASE LIST:

7. Why are these corridos your favorite ones? PLEASE EXPLAIN:

8. Do you live in

___ El Paso
___ Juárez
___ Other: _____

Thank you for your time.

Appendix 2. Spanish Texts of Corridos and Narcocorridos

The following Spanish texts of corridos and narcocorridos appear in the order they are presented in the book. Translations come from the original source (e.g., Arhoolie Records) or were made by my translation assistants and me.

EL CORRIDO DE GREGORIO CORTEZ

Pedro Rocha/Lupe Martínez, October 1929 (Arhoolie Records)

En el condado del Carmen
miren lo que ha sucedido
Murió el sherife mayor
quedando Román herido

Otro día por la mañana
cuando la gente llegó
Unos a los otros dicen
no saben quien lo mató

Se anduvieron informando
como tres horas después,
Supieron que el malhechor
era Gregorio Cortez

Insortaron a Cortez
por toditito el estado
Vivo o muerto que se aprehenda
porque a varios ha matado.

Decía Gregorio Cortez
con su pistola en la mano

"No siento haberlo matado
lo que siento es a mi hermano."

Decía Gregorio Cortez
con su alma muy encendida
"No siento haberlo matado
la defensa es permitida."

Venían los americanos
que por el viento volaban,
porque se iban a ganar
tres mil pesos que les daban.

Siguió con rumbo a González,
varios sherifes lo vieron
no lo quisieron seguir
porque le tuvieron miedo.

Venían los perros jaunes
venían sobre la huella
Pero alcanzar a Cortez
era alcanzar a una estrella.

Decía Gregorio Cortez
"Pa'qué se valen de planes,
si no pueden agarrarme.
Ni con esos perros jaunes."

Decían los americanos
"Si lo vemos que le haremos
si le entramos por derecho
muy poquitos volveremos."

En el redondel del rancho
lo alcanzaron a rodear,
Poquitos mas trescientos
y allí les brincó el corral.

Allá por Encinal
o según por lo que dicen
Se agarraron a balazos
y les mató otro sherife.

Decía Gregorio Cortez
con su pistola en su mano,
"No corran rinches cobardes
con un solo mexicano."

Giró con rumbo a Laredo
sin ninguna timidez,
"¡Síganme rinches cobardes,
yo soy Gregorio Cortez!"

Gregorio le dice a Juan
en el rancho del Ciprés,
"Platícame qué hay de nuevo,
yo soy Gregorio Cortez."

Gregorio le dice a Juan,
"Muy pronto lo vas a ver,
anda háblale a los sherifes
que me vengan a aprender."

Cuando llegan los sherifes
Gregorio se presentó,
"Por la buena si me llevan
porque de otro modo no."

Ya agarraron a Cortez
ya terminó la cuestión,
la pobre de su familia
la lleva en el corazón.

Ya con esto me despido
con la sombra de un Ciprés,
aquí se acaba cantando
la tragedia de Cortez.

"El Corrido de Gregorio Cortez," performed by Pedro Rocha and Lupe Martinez, October 1929, from Arhoolie Records (www.arhoolie.com) collection CD #7019/20, *Corridos y Tragedias de la Frontera.*

(CORRIDO DE) JOAQUÍN MURIETA

As recorded in Herrera-Sobek (1993), Sonnichsen (1975)

Yo no soy americano
pero comprendo el inglés.
Yo lo aprendí con mi hermano
al derecho y al revés
A cualquier americano
lo hago temblar a mis pies.

Cuando apenas era un niño
huérfano a mi me dejaron.
Nadie me hizo ni un cariño,
a mi hermano lo mataron,
Y a mi esposa Carmelita,
cobardes la asesinaron.

Yo me vine de Hermosillo
en busca de oro y riqueza.
Al indio pobre y sencillo
lo defendí con fiereza
Y a buen precio los sherifes
pagaban por mi cabeza.

A los ricos avarientos,
yo les quité su dinero.
Con los humildes y pobres
yo me quité mi sombrero.
Ay, que leyes tan injustas
fue llamarme bandolero.

A Murieta no le gusta
lo que hace no es desmentir.
Vengo a vengar a mi esposa,
y lo vuelvo a repetir,
Carmelita tan hermosa,
como la hicieron sufrir.

Por cantinas me metí,
castigando americanos.
"Tú serás el capitán
que mataste a mi hermano.

Lo agarraste indefenso,
orgulloso americano."

Mi carrera comenzó
por una escena terrible.
Cuando llegué a setecientos
ya mi nombre era temible.
Cuando llegué a mil doscientos
ya mi nombre era terrible.

Yo soy aquel que domina
hasta leones africanos.
Por eso salgo al camino
a matar americanos.
Ya no es otro mi destino
¡Pon cuidado, parroquianos!

Las pistolas y las dagas
son juguetes para mi.
Balazos y puñaladas,
carcajadas para mi.
Ahora con medios cortados
ya se asustan por aquí.

No soy chileno ni extraño
en este suelo que piso.
De México es California,
porque Dios así lo quiso,
y en mi sarape cosida
traigo mi fe de bautismo.

Qué bonito es California
con sus calles alineadas,
donde paseaba Murieta
con su tropa bien formada,
con su pistola repleta,
y su montura plateada.

Me he paseado en California
por el año del cincuenta,
Con mi montura plateada,
y mi pistola repleta,

Yo soy ese mexicano
de nombre Joaquín Murieta.

CONTRABANDISTAS TEQUILEROS (LIQUOR SMUGGLERS)

Pedro Rocha/Lupe Martínez, 1930 (Arhoolie Records)

En mil novecientos treinta,
señores pon atención,
en la cárcel de Del Río
fue trovada esta canción.

De la cárcel de Del Río
ni me quisiera acordar,
Que el diecisiete de marzo
nos iban a sentenciar.

Nos sacaron de la cárcel
derecho a la Calle Real,
Y nos dice el Colorado
ya los voy a retratar.

Luego que nos retrataron
a la cárcel nos llevaron,
Sin saber nuestra sentencia
porque no nos la explicaron.

Bonita cárcel en Del Río
pero a mí no me consuela,
Porque dan puros frijoles
y un platito de avena.

Bonita cárcel en Del Río
pero aun no se puede creer,
Son contados los amigos
que te quieren ir a ver.

"Joaquin Murieta," as it appears in Herrera-Sobek 1993. Original recording/transcription by Phillip Sonnichsen (1975), as performed by Los Madrugadores, from Arhoolie Records (www.arhoolie.com) collection CD #7019/20, *Corridos y Tragedias de la Frontera.*

Yo les digo a mis amigos
cuando vayan a pasar,
Fíjense en los denunciantes,
no los vayan a entregar.

Yo les digo a mis amigos
cuando estén al otro lado,
Fíjense en las veredas
por donde va el Colorado.

Quizá ya en el Naqueví
aprehende a un compañero,
Que vendió a un denunciante
el día treinta de enero.

Fíjate bien denunciante
porque lo estoy diciendo,
Que por amor al dinero
nos estuvistes vendiendo.

Pero de eso no hay cuidado,
ni tampoco hay que pensar,
Vamos a tomar cerveza
y en seguida a vacilar.

Pero de eso no hay cuidado,
ya lo que pasó voló,
Por causa de un denunciante,
preso aquí me encuentro yo.

Yo anduve en muchas parrandas
con amigos en buenos carros,
Y hoy me llevan prisionero
ni quien me traiga un cigarro.

Ya no llores mamacita,
te llevo en mi corazón,
Por entrarle al contrabando
me lleva la prohibición.

Entiéndanlo amigos míos
y pongan mucha atención,

Por andar vendiendo el trago
nos llevan a Leavenworth.

La máquina del S.P.
Corre con mucha violencia,
Y se lleva los convictos
derecho a la penitencia.

Estos versos son compuestos
por toditos en reunión
Unos por el contrabando
y otros por la inmigración.

Adiós mi madre querida,
solo tú lloras mis penas,
Y nos llevan prisioneros
mancornados con cadena.

Adiós mi madre querida
me voy a la penitencia,
Cuando salga nos veremos,
si el Señor me da licencia.

Adiós cárcel de Del Río,
adiós torres y campanas,
Adiós todos mis amigos,
adiós lindas mexicanas.

Los que viven en Del Río
gozan de tranquilidad,
Porque ellos toman tequila
con mucha facilidad.

Ya con ésta me despido,
porque siento mucho frío,
Aquí se acaba cantando,
del contrabando Del Río.

"Contrabandistas Tequileros," performed by Pedro Rocha and Lupe Martinez, 1930, from Arhoolie Records (www.arhoolie.com) collection CD #7019/20, *Corridos y Tragedias de la Frontera*.

CORRIDO DE LOS BOOTLEGGERS

Francisco Montalvo/Andres Berlanga, 1935 (Arhoolie Records)

Pongan cuidado señores,
lo que aquí voy a cantarles,
Me puse a rifar mi suerte
con catorce federales.

Me puse a pensar señores
que trabajo ya no había,
Tenía que buscar mi vida
si el Señor me concedía.

Ya la siembra no da nada
no me queda que decirles,
Ahora la mejor cosecha
es la que dan los barriles.

Toda la gente que siembra
hasta el año venidero,
Ahora no son los barriles
todo es que salga el primero.

Los que están cociendo el trago
a nadie les piden mal,
Pero van y los denuncian
y le traen la federal.

Cuando iban a entregar el trago
con peligro y muy barato,
No más me echo dos o tres tragos
y el miedo es no más un rato.

Mientras sigan las cantinas
así seguirá pasando,
Porque el pobre esté en la cárcel
y el rico se ande gozando.

Pero el hijo no hace caso,
antes que lo hallan pescado,
La madre es la que sufre
cuando el hijo está encerrado.

Mi madre se encuentra triste,
mi padre con más razón,
De ver a su hijo encerrado
en esta triste prisión.

Pobrecita de mi madre,
a que suerte le ha tocado,
En las puertas de esta cárcel
lágrimas se le han rodado.

Mi madre muy afanada
hablando con el abogado,
A ver si me saca en fiancé
de la cárcel del condado.

Yo era bootlegga de marca
porque no me habían pescado,
Porque todos mis entregos
los hacía con cuidado.

Aquí en este San Antonio,
todos los alrededores,
nunca pescan los bootlegga
nomás los trabajadores.

Cuando llegamos allá
me decían muy seguidito,
"Aquí en esta penitencia
los sentencian sin delito."

El que compuso estos versos
no es compositor de marca,
En el centro de este disco,
su nombre como se llama.

Ahí les va la despedida
no me lo tengan a mal,
Cuidado con los barriles
porque cae la federal.

"Corrido de los Bootleggers," performed by Francisco Montalvo and Andres Berlanga, August 15, 1935, from Arhoolie Records (www.arhoolie.com) collection CD #7019/20, *Corridos y Tragedias de la Frontera.*

EL TARASCO (THE TARASCAN)

Los Tigres del Norte

Primero me dieron alas
y ahora me quieren parar
y no soy mono de alambre
Que cuerda le pueden dar
Yo no soy Juan Colorado
Pero soy de Michoacán

¿Cuánto costará la sierra
de Michoacán a Colima?
Yo traigo entre ceja y ceja
El aguaje de Aguilillas
Allí los gallos son finos
Y las muchachas bonitas

Ya no gasten en radares
Ni destrozando mis pistas
Yo soy un ave nocturna
Que atteriza en cualquier milpa
Además el día que caiga
Caerán muchos de allá arriba

Mescaron de chirona
Porque así les convenía
Ya les vino grande el saco
Y me borran de la lista
Al llegar de Redwood City
Yo les pago la visita

Por unos dedos traidores
Tuve un fracaso en Uruapán
También mi linda borrada
Me falló alla por Sahuayo
Yo soy tarasco efectivo
Pronto les daré su pago

Ya no gasten en radares
Ni destrozando mis pistas
Yo soy un ave nocturna
Que aterriza en cualquier milpa

Además el día que caiga
Caerán muchos de allá arriba

LOS TRES DE LA SIERRA (THE THREE MEN FROM THE SIERRA)

Los Norteños de Ojinaga

Órale mi güero, levanté toda la gente
Una noche de tormenta, en una brecha en la sierra
Kiko llevaba a su gente a levanter la cosecha
A recoger oro verde que ese año le dió la tierra

Armando lleva la troca una Ram era del año
No saben gringos malditos por las que estamos pasando
Para llevarles la droga que a ustedes les gusta tanto

Dice sonriendo Rubén, miren ya vamos llegando
Mientras bufava la gris que en la caja iban llenado,
De elodo y agua los hombres dicen total bien armados

Que chulas se ven las matas en el fondo de la sierra
Más chulas se ven las pacas de dólares cuando llegan
Que Kiko alegre comparte con la ley y con su gente

Se ven los tres de la sierra en sus troconas del año
En la frontera los vemos sus negocios vigilando
Y allá en un rancho en la sierra la cosecha se está dando

No hay otro, lleva por nombre en la sierra esa gran rancho
Francisco, Rubén y Armando ya están moviendo sus hombres
Ya los esperan con ancias con bravor y corredores

EL GENERAL (THE GENERAL)

Los Tigres del Norte

Un general ha caído
Dijo la televisión

Cuando le dijeron el puesto
Pensaron que era el mejor
Por culpa del contrabando
Ahora está en la prisión

En Culiacán y Jalisco
Le pidieron protección
Le ofrecieron buenas cosas
La prensa así lo anunció
Viviendo con tanto lujo
Se hizo la investigación

Aquellos grandes embarques
Y no podrán transitar
Quien les echaba la mano
Ahora está en el penal
Y en la baja California
Cayó otro general

Según las declaraciones
Las que decía el general
Que al señor de los cielos
Siempre lo quiso agarrar
Y que lo hizo su amigo
Por su confianza ganar

Con un millón de los verdes
No lo pudieron comprar
Al delegado en Tijuana
Al valiente federal
Hay gente que su trabajo lo
Quiere y sabe cuidar

A diferentes países los certifican los gringos
No quieren que exista droga
Pues dicen que es un peligro
"Díganme, quién certifica
A los Estados Unidos?"

Para agarrar a los narcos
México ha sido derecho
Los gringos compran la coca
La pagan a cualquier precio

No quieren que exista droga
Pero se dan privilegio

JESÚS AMADO

Los Tigres del Norte

Jiménez su apelativo
Su nombre Jesús Amado
Peleó con la policía
De Brownsville en el Río Bravo
No le quitaron la carga
Por ser un gallo jugado.

Como las once del día
Hicieron una llamada
Que en una cámara de hule
Su contrabando pasaba
Que Amado lo cruzaría
A las dos de la mañana

Un reflector lo alumbró
Y varios tiros se oyeron
Amado les contestó
Con su perki y con un cuerno
Matando a dos policías
Los otros cinco corrieron

Cuando volvió a Sinaloa
Le puso precio al soplón
Llevándose una sorpresa
Cuando le dieron razón
Una mujer que tenía
Le preparó la traición

Cuando le fue a reclamar
Amado sintió un balazo
Pero también disparó
A donde vió el fogonazo
Muy mal herida Patricia
Rendida cayó en sus brazos

Antes de morir le dijo
Lo hice porque te quiero
Sabía que andabas con otra
Y no aguantaba los celos
Deseaba mirarte muerto
Que verte en brazos ajenos

CONTRABANDO Y TRAICIÓN (CONTRABAND AND BETRAYAL)

Los Tigres del Norte

Salieron de San Isidro, procedentes a Tijuana
Traían la llanta del carro, repletas de hierba mala
Eran Emilio Varela y Camelia la Tejana

Pasaron por San Clemente, los pararon la emigración
Les pidió sus documentos, les dijo de donde son
Ella era de San Antonio, una hembra de corazón

Una hembra si quiere un hombre, por él puede dar la vida
Pero hay que tener cuidado si esa hembra se siente herida
La traición y el contrabando son cosas incompartidas

A Los Ángeles llegaron a Hollywood se pasaron
En un callejón oscuro, las cuatro llantas cambiaron
Ahí entregaron la hierba, y allí también les pagaron

Emilio dice a Camelia, hoy te das por despedida
Con la parte que te toca tú puedes rehacer tu vida
Yo me voy pa San Francisco, con la dueña de mi vida

Sonaron siete balazos, Camelia a Emilio mataba
La policía solo halló una pistola tirada
Del dinero y Camelia, nunca más se supo nada

MIS TRES ANIMALES (MY THREE ANIMALS)

Los Tucanes de Tijuana

Vivo de tres animales
Que quiero como a mi vida
con ellos gano dinero
y ni les compro comida.
Son animales cretinos
Mi perico, mi gallo y mi chiva.

En California y Nevada
en Tejas y en Arizona
también allá en Chicago
tengo unas cuantas personas
que venden mis animales
más que hamburguesas
en el McDonald's.

Aprendí a vivir la vida
hasta que tuve dinero
y no niego que fui pobre
tampoco que fui burrero.
Ahora soy un gran señor,
mis mascotas codician los hueros.

Traigo cerquita la muerte
pero no me se rajar.
Sé que me busca el gobierno
hasta debajo del mar.
Pero para todo hay maña,
mi escondite no han podido hallar.

El dinero en abundancia
también es muy peligroso.
Por eso yo me lo gasto
con mis amigos gustosos
y las mujeres la neta
ven dinero y se le salen los ojos.

Dicen que mis animales
van a acabar con la gente.
Pero no es obligación

que se les pongan enfrente.
Mis animales son bravos,
si no saben toriar pues no le entren.

ME GUSTA PONERLE AL POLVO (I LIKE TO DO COCAINE)

Exterminador

Me gustan acciones fuertes, me gusta pegarle al polvo
Sé que me andan buscando, y que a mucho les estorbo

Ando detrás de la muerte, por la forma en que me porto
Me gustan acciones fuertes, me gusta ponerle al polvo
Ya sé que me andan buscando, y que a muchos les estorbo

Me andan siguiendo los pasos, ya ni a gusto me paseo
Por ahí en algunos lugares, algunos me miran feo
Ya sé que a mis enemigos yo les gusto para trofeo

En el rancho El Zapatío, tengo una rubia preciosa
Muy seguido voy a verla, me gusta por cariñosa
Es bonita y presumida y la voy a hacer mi esposa

A todos los que me buscan, un consejo voy a darles
El gusto se lleva dentro, y yo quiero recordarles
Me gusta gozar la vida y el dinero es pa'gastarse

Ya con esta me despido, me gusta ser muy parejo
Potranca que no sea mía, yo se la bajo a su dueño
Soy amigo de los hombres y a ninguno me le rajo

EL TORO BRAVO (THE ANGRY BULL)

Los Truenos de Sinaloa

Abran el paso señores
que aquí les vengo a cantar

un corrido a un toro bravo
porque es un amigo leal
Es del rancho Los Cortijos
cerquita de Coloacal.

Aunque es un hombre tranquilo
yo les regalo un consejo
no le tapen el camino
si quieren llegar a viejos
cuando a un toro se provoca
la muerte no anda muy lejos.

Señores, el toro bravo
siempre carga bien fajada
una 38 super,
con cachas de oro adornadas
Siempre que se le ha ofrecido
no se ha quedado callada.

No cierren esas veredas porque
por ahí viaja un hombre
Nadie sabe lo que lleva
pa' que saber lo que esconde? y
a muchos por saberlo
se han muerto y ya no responden.

(Arriba Sinaloa, Copamavel. El RV)

Para brillar las estrellas
Para calentar el sol
Para gastarse el dinero
Para ganarlo el valor
Para amistades sinceras
el toro bravo señor.

Jamás le falta el dinero
las cosas le salen bien
le sobra la inteligencia
cumple bien con su deber
Cuando se hacen bien las cosas
se vive mejor que un rey.

Que revolcaba aquel agua
ningún camarón se ve.
Manuel es el toro bravo
un hombre de mucha ley
Adiós hombres de la sierra
los saluda el RV.

EL GALLO JUGADO (THE ROOSTER PLAYER)

Los Cuacos del Norte

Andan diciendo por ahí
que me van a dar de tiros
que porque soy mujeriego
y por negocios prohibidos
yo sé que hay muchos que quieren
arrecortarme el camino.

Si traigo billetes verdes
es porque ando en el peligro
no le temo a los balazos
yo traigo un cuerno de chivo
y él que no lo quiera creer
que le brinque a lo barrido.

Si se trata de mujeres
me gusta rifar mi suerte
no le temo a los balazos
traigo con que defenderme
la muerte ha de ser bonita
si me matan frente a frente.

Me gusta jalar la banda
al estilo Sinaloa
que me hechen puros corridos
y que suene la tambora.
Soy de los gallos jugados
donde se da la amapola.

Los que andan en el negocio
nunca se deben confiar
porque hasta el mejor amigo
bien los puede traicionar
y lo mandan al pantión
ó acabas en el penal.

A los que quieren matarme
yo les quiero aconsejar
es mejor que no me busquen
porque me van a encontrar
y mi cuernito de chivo
lo voy a hacer rebuznar.

Este trabajo es bonito y no
lo pienso dejar porque
me sobran mujeres y
dinero pa' gastar.
Pero esto si es peligroso,
por si alguno quiere entrar.

EL ZORRO DE OJINAGA (THE FOX OF OJINAGA)

Los Tigres del Norte

El cuidaba la frontera, por órdenes del Tío Sam
Y cazaba terroristas de esos que saben matar
El Zorro de Ojinaga, Pablo Acosta Villareal

Pero viene otra consigna, dijeron a publicar
Dicen que bajaba aviones con polvo pa comenzar
Como el hombre ya está muerto ya no lo desmentirán

La confianza y prepotencia es la falla del valiente
No te fíes de los alagos, ni siquiera a parientes
A los Zorros más astutos, los atrapan con su gente

En el cielo de Arizona, lo quisieron derribar
Le mandó a Vecías, dicen con motor mirage
Pero el zorro con su Cessna, hizo a Diablo quedar mal

Le mataron a su hermano que era su mano derecha
Y después allá en el rancho también cobraron la renta
Como el hombre ya está muerto ni modo que lo desmientan

PACAS DE A KILO (KILO SACKS)

Los Tigres del Norte

Me gusta andar por la sierra, me crié entre los matorales
Allí aprendí a hacer las cuentas, nomás contando costales
Me gusta burlar las redes, que tienden los federales

Muy pegadito a la sierra, tengo un rancho ganadero
Ganados sin garrapatas, que llevo pal extranjero
Que chulas se ven mis vacas, con colitas de borrego

El Tigre a mi me acompaña, porque ha sido un gran amigo
Maestro en la pista chica, además muy precavido
Él sabe que en esta chamba, no es bueno volar dormido

Por el negocio que tengo, por donde quiera me paseo
No me gusta que presumen, tampoco me miren feo
Me gusta que me platiquen, pero no todo les creo

Por ahí andan platicando, que un día me van a matar
No me asustan las culebras, yo sé perder y ganar
Ahí traigo un cuerno de chivo, para él que le quiera entrar

Adiós tierra de Coahuila, de Sinaloa y Durango
De Sonora y Tamaulipas, Chihuahua te andas quedando
Si me quieren conocer, en Juárez me ando paseando

Notes

Prologue

1. From diaries and notes of Woody Guthrie included in a special exhibit at the Smithsonian Institution's National Museum of American History, summer, 2000.

2. The word "Kermess" has European origins, often referring to a church or charitable festival. It was, however, the term used by the community for this festival.

3. Maquilas represent globalism close to home. They include assembly plants and other industries on the Mexican side of the border that employ low-cost Mexican labor and are usually owned by foreign corporations whose headquarters and primary operations are elsewhere.

4. An ejido is a traditional communal farm, once a staple of land reform programs in Mexico.

Chapter 1

1. However, it would be overly facile to cast this as a totalizing explanation. The addicts on this corner or any corner are there for a complex of reasons, some individual, some structural. And there are plenty of addicts who are not on the corner, but are lawyers in the courtroom or doctors in the office, though the narratives surrounding their use may be substantially different.

2. I use the term "social strata" with a clear awareness that it is an artifice, that social strata are not clearly bounded social entities. Nevertheless, as long as this is understood, it remains a convenient device for this discussion.

3. It is not clear how Gramsci defines "group."

4. I am using "aggregations" instead of "system."

5. That is, they share a similar constellation of economic, social, cultural, and symbolic capital, said by Bourdieu (1986, 1987) to be the factors that "together empower (or otherwise) agents in their struggle for position within 'social space'" (see Crompton 1993, p. 173).

Chapter 2

1. The term "archetype" as I use it is different from the Jungian concept of archetype, which refers to archetypes existing in the collective unconscious (Jung 1959). Archetypes in the cultural sense, as I use the term, are part of what would be viewed as the "collective conscious."

2. Other groups, perhaps not quite so famous, include Exterminador and Los Capos de México (considered "hard core" according to one review; see Kun 1997), Los Huracanes del Norte, Los Dinámicos del Norte, and Los Rebeldes de Tijuana.

3. The "corrido community" refers to the hypothetical community of people who listen to and produce corridos and who participate in and understand the "cosmological orientation" expressed in them. This hypothesized community is a community in the broad sense, and not necessarily bound to a specific place.

4. According to McDowell (1981), Paredes defines a parranda as a kind of mobile or "ambulatory" cantina (Paredes 1976, p. xxii).

5. This version was performed by Pedro Rocha and Lupe Martínez, October 1929, and is from the Arhoolie Records collection entitled *Corridos y Tragedias de la Frontera: First Recordings of Historic Mexican-American Ballads (1928–37)*. The words are similar to the version cited by Paredes (1976). The Spanish text of all corridos discussed in this book appears in Appendix 2.

6. From Herrera-Sobek 1993; Sonnichsen 1975.

7. Note that this corrido is presented in the first person—not as a song *about*, but as a song *by*. In this form it has more of the boasting quality that is found in some corridos of this genre, including narcocorridos. A question: When corridos are sung in this manner, does the *corridista*, or singer, "become" (in this case) Joaquín Murieta?

8. This version was sung by Pedro Rocha and Lupe Martínez in 1930, and is taken from the Arhoolie Records compilation entitled *Corridos y Tragedias de la Frontera: First Recordings of Historic Mexican-American Ballads (1928–37)*. It is different from the version cited by Paredes (1976). This translation is mine, based on the booklet and translations accompanying the compilation.

9. This version is also taken from the Arhoolie corrido compilation *Corridos y Tragedias de la Frontera: First Recordings of Historic Mexican-American Ballads (1928–37)*, and is sung by Francisco Montalvo and Andrés Berlanga, recorded at the Texas Hotel, San Antonio, August 15, 1935.

10. As a side note, I have encountered numerous words in "border Spanish" (or *calo*) that begin with or contain the phoneme "ch" (e.g., the name "Chalino," the state of Chihuahua, the word *"chavo"* for young person, the word *"cheve"* for beer). I am curious as to whether this phoneme itself imparts a sense of power or strength into the word itself, or the performance of the word—in the manner that power is construed in the northern Mexico region.

Chapter 3

1. These and other narcocorridos were translated with the significant assistance of Rafael Núñez, a journalist working on both sides of the border in El Paso/Juárez, who is very familiar with the code words and double entendres found in what might be called "narcodiscourse." Lori and Martin Tapia, members of a well-known norteño band based in Douglas, Arizona, also provided significant assistance with specific translations.

2. See list of phrases and terminology later in this chapter.

3. This warning deserves note because it is so close in tone to attitudes and beliefs I have encountered elsewhere in street research projects, in which drug use is cast as an issue of mastery or something that one must prove one can handle.

4. From a compilation entitled *Puros Corridos Perrones*, produced by Cintas Acuario in Los Angeles, California.

5. Translated and explained by Joshua Herrera of El Paso, Texas.

6. Emphasis on "sometimes." To suggest that all who dress in chero style are narcotraffickers or want to be narcotraffickers would be extreme stereotyping.

7. Not, of course, an official canonized saint, but a "people's saint," as it were.

8. This mirrors what was said by one of the adult listener respondents, as noted above.

9. There is, I heard, a popular corrido about the cell phone, a spoof. It is a story of a man going out on a first dinner date who is trying to impress the woman. He has his cell phone with him and has a friend call him during dinner so that he can appear to have important doings.

Chapter 4

1. I say "for the most part" because, as I have mentioned, there is that subset among the more privileged for whom the narcotrafficker life has an appeal, for its thrills, its danger, its opportunity to make a name—or a "legend"—for oneself outside the approved social boundaries of the elite as a rebel of sorts.

2. *The Ballad of Gregorio Cortez*, directed by Robert Young, starring Edward James Olmos, and based on the work of Américo Paredes.

3. My use is also distinguished from its usage by Cornel West (1989) in reference to "a distinctive feature of black styles . . . a certain projection of self—more a *persona*—in performance."

4. My thanks to Dr. Dell Hymes for this reference and the general point of comparison to other hero tales.

5. In another context, see Liebow (1993) on this sentiment among homeless women.

6. I might note, for example, that in Mexico, on Good Friday (before Easter Sunday), figures of Judas Iscariot are sometimes burned, along with other figures representing popular or moral enemies, antagonists, or per-

sons subject to popular opprobrium. A perennial favorite for burning is Uncle Sam.

Appendix 1

1. Defined by McDowell (1981, p. 45) as the "hypothesized human community which supports an active ballad tradition while providing the cosmological orientation represented in those ballads."

References

Agar, M. 1973. *Ripping and Running: A Formal Ethnology of Urban Addicts.* New York: Seminar Press.

Anderson, B. 1983. *Imagined Communities: Reflections on the Origin and Spread of Nationalism.* London: Verso.

Anderson, E. 1992. "The Story of John Turner." In A. V. Harrell and G. E. Peterson, eds., *Drugs, Crime, and Social Isolation,* pp. 147–179. Washington, D.C.: Urban Institute Press.

Anderson, N. [1923] 1961. *The Hobo.* Chicago: University of Chicago Press.

Aramoni, A. 1965. *Psicoanálisis de la dinámica de un pueblo.* Mexico City: B. Costa-Amic.

Astorga, L. 1997. "Los corridos de traficantes de drogas en México y Colombia." *Revista Mexicana de Sociología* 59 (4): 245–261.

Bakhtin, M. M. 1981. *The Dialogic Imagination.* Edited by M. Holquist. Translated by M. Holquist and C. Emerson. Austin: University of Texas Press.

Bandura, A. 1986. *Social Foundations of Thought and Action: A Social-Cognitive View.* Englewood Cliffs, N.J.: Prentice-Hall.

Barriga, M. D. 1997. "The Culture of Poverty as Relajo." *Aztlán* 22 (2): 43–65.

Barthes, R. 1972. *Mythologies.* Translated by Annette Lavers. New York: Hill and Wang.

Battaglia, D., ed. 1995. *Rhetorics of Self-Making.* Berkeley and Los Angeles: University of California Press.

Bauman, R. 1986. "Performance and Honor in Thirteenth-Century Iceland." *Journal of American Folklore* 99 (392): 131–150.

———. 1993. Introduction to A. Paredes, *Folklore and Culture on the Texas-Mexican Border.* Edited by R. Bauman, pp. ix–xxiii. Austin: Center for Mexican American Studies, University of Texas at Austin.

Bauman, R., and R. D. Abrahams, eds. 1981. *"And Other Neighborly Names": Social Process and Cultural Image in Texas Folklore.* Austin: University of Texas Press.

Bernard, H. R. 1988. *Research Methods in Cultural Anthropology.* Thousand Oaks, Calif.: Sage.

Berreman, G. D., and K. M. Zaretsky. 1981. *Social Inequality: Comparative and Developmental Approaches.* New York: Academic Press.

Bourdieu, P. 1973. "Cultural Reproduction and Social Reproduction." In R. Brown, ed., *Knowledge, Education, and Cultural Change.* London: Tavistock.

———. 1977. *Outline of a Theory of Practice.* Cambridge: Cambridge University Press.

———. 1986. *Distinction: A Social Critique of the Judgement of Taste.* New York: Routledge.

———. 1987. "What Makes a Social Class?" *Berkeley Journal of Sociology* 22: 762.

Bourgois, Phillipe. 1989. "In Search of Horatio Alger: Culture and Ideology in the Crack Economy." *Contemporary Drug Problems* 16 (4): 619–650.

———. 1996. *In Search of Respect: Selling Crack in El Barrio.* Cambridge: Cambridge University Press.

Carrithers, M., S. Collins, and S. Lukes, eds. 1985. *The Category of the Person: Anthropology, Philosophy, History.* Cambridge: Cambridge University Press.

Collier, R. 1997. "Drugs Muscle into Mexican Music Mix: Trafficking Theme Hits Popular Nerve." *San Francisco Chronicle,* October 17, p. A-1.

Crompton, R. 1993. *Class and Stratification: An Introduction to Current Debates.* Cambridge, Eng.: Polity Press.

De Sousa, R. 1990. *The Rationality of Emotion.* Cambridge, Mass.: MIT Press.

DeVos, George, and Manuel Suárez-Orozco. 1990. *Status Inequality: The Self in Culture.* Newbury Park, Calif.: Sage.

Dumont, L. 1980. *Homo Hierarchicus: The Caste System and Its Implications.* Rev. ed. Chicago: University of Chicago Press.

———. 1986. *Essays on Individualism: Modern Ideology in Anthropological Perspective.* Chicago: University of Chicago Press.

Dwyer, A. 1994. *On the Line: Life on the U.S.-Mexican Border.* London: Latin America Bureau.

Edberg, M. 1998. "Street Cuts: Splices from Project Notebooks and Other Indelible Impressions." *Anthropology and Humanism* 23 (1) (June 1998).

Epstein, D. 1972. *The Genesis and Function of Squatter Settlements in Brasilia.* The Anthropology of Urban Environments, Society for Applied Anthropology Monograph Series, no. 11. Washington, D.C.: Society for Applied Anthropology.

Fanon, F. 1968. *The Wretched of the Earth.* New York: Grove Press.

Fatemi, K. 1990. Introduction to K. Fatemi, ed., *The Maquiladora Industry: Economic Solution or Problem?* pp. 3–18. New York: Praeger.

Fleisher, M. S. 1998. *Dead End Kids: Gang Girls and the Boys They Know.* Madison: University of Wisconsin Press.

Foster, G. M. 1967. *Tzintzuntzán: Mexican Peasants in a Changing World.* Boston: Little, Brown.

Foucault, M. 1972. *The Archaeology of Knowledge.* Translated by A. M. Sheridan Smith. New York: Harper Colophon.

———. 1973. *Madness and Civilization: A History of Insanity in the Age of Reason.* Translated by R. Howard. New York: Vintage/Random House.

———. 1975. *The Birth of the Clinic: An Archaeology of Medical Perception*. Translated by A. M. Sheridan Smith. New York: Vintage/Random House.

———. 1979. *Discipline and Punish: The Birth of the Prison*. Translated by A. Sheridan. New York: Vintage/Random House.

———. 1980a. *The History of Sexuality*. Vol. 1, *An Introduction*. Translated by R. Hurley. New York: Vintage/Random House.

———. 1980b. *Power/Knowledge: Selected Interviews and Other Writings, 1972–1977*. Edited by C. Gordon. Translated by C. Gordon, L. Marshall, J. Mepham, and K. Soper. New York: Pantheon Books.

García Torres, G. 1997. "Los corridos de Inés Chávez García: Lírica de una leyenda moderna." *Aztlán* 22 (1): 49–71.

Geertz, C. 1983. *Local Knowledge: Further Essays in Interpretive Anthropology*. New York: Basic Books.

Gilroy, P. 1993. *The Black Atlantic: Modernity and Double Consciousness*. Cambridge: Harvard University Press.

Gmelch, G., and W. P. Zenner. 1996. *Urban Life: Readings in Urban Anthropology*. 3d ed. Prospect Heights, Ill.: Waveland Press.

Goffman, E. 1959. *The Presentation of Self in Everyday Life*. New York: Doubleday/Anchor.

Goldwert, M. 1985. "Mexican Machismo: The Flight from Femininity." *Psychoanalytic Review* 72: 161–169.

Goode, J., and E. Eames. 1996. "An Anthropological Critique of the Culture of Poverty." In G. Gmelch and W. P. Zenner, eds., *Urban Life: Readings in Urban Anthropology*, 3d ed., pp. 405–417. Prospect Heights, Ill.: Waveland Press.

Gramsci, A. 1971. *Selections from the Prison Notebooks*. London: Lawrence and Wishart.

Grusky, D. B., ed. 1994. *Social Stratification in Sociological Perspective*. Boulder, Colo.: Westview.

Hall, S. [1989] 1995. "New Ethnicities." In B. Ashcroft, G. Griffins, and H. Tiffin, eds., *The Post-Colonial Studies Reader*, pp. 223–227. London: Routledge.

Hankiss, A. 1981. "Ontologies of the Self: On the Mythological Rearranging of One's Life History." In D. Bertaux, ed., *Biography and Society: The Life History Approach in the Social Sciences*, pp. 203–209. Beverly Hills, Calif.: Sage.

Hannerz, U. 1980. *Exploring the City: Inquiries toward an Urban Anthropology*. New York: Columbia University Press.

———. 1987. "The World of Creolization." *Africa* 57 (4): 546–559.

———. 1989. "Culture between Center and Periphery: Toward a Macroanthropology." *Ethnos* 54: 200–216.

Helms, M. 1979. *Ancient Panama: Chiefs in Search of Power*. Austin: University of Texas Press.

Hernández, G. 1992. "El corrido ayer y hoy: Nuevas notas para su estudio." In J. M. Valenzuela Arce, ed., *Entre la magia y la historia: Tradiciones, mitos y leyendas de la frontera*. Tijuana, Mex.: El Colegio de la Frontera Norte.

Herrera-Sobek, M. 1979. "The Theme of Drug Smuggling in the Mexican Corrido." *Revista Chicano-Riqueña* 7 (4): 49–61.

———. 1990. *The Mexican Corrido: A Feminist Analysis*. Bloomington: Indiana University Press.

———. 1993. *Northward Bound: The Mexican Immigrant Experience in Ballad and Song*. Bloomington: Indiana University Press.

Hobsbawm, E. 1969. *Bandits*. New York: Delacorte Press.

———. 1990. *Nations and Nationalism: Programme, Myth, Reality*. Cambridge: Cambridge University Press.

Holland, D., et al. 1998. *Identity and Agency in Cultural Worlds*. Cambridge: Harvard University Press.

Hymes, D. 1974. *Foundations of Sociolinguistics: An Ethnographic Approach*. Philadelphia: University of Pennsylvania Press.

Inkeles, A., and D. H. Smith. 1964. *Becoming Modern: Individual Change in Six Developing Countries*. Cambridge: Harvard University Press.

Jung, C. G. 1959. *The Archetypes and the Collective Unconscious*. New York: Bollingen Foundation/Princeton University Press.

Kaplan, R. D. 1998. "Travels into America's Future: Mexico and the Southwest." *Atlantic Monthly*, July, 47–68.

Katz, F. 1998. *The Life and Times of Pancho Villa*. Stanford: Stanford University Press.

Kearney, M. November 1998. "The Classificatory and Value Filtering Power of Borders." Paper presented at American Anthropological Association Annual Meeting, Philadelphia.

Kun, J. 1997. "Narcocorridistas," *Village Voice*, December 2, p. 67.

Labov, W. 1966. *The Social Stratification of English in New York City*. Washington, D.C.: Center for Applied Linguistics.

———. 1972. *Language in the Inner City: Studies in Black English Vernacular*. Philadelphia: University of Pennsylvania Press.

Leenhardt, M. [1947] 1979. *Do Kamo: Person and Myth in the Melanesian World*. Chicago: University of Chicago Press.

León, I., and R. Bedoya. 1983. "Cultura popular y cultura masiva en el México contemporáneo: Conversaciones con Carlos Monsiváis." *Diálogos* 19.

Levinson, S. C. 1983. *Pragmatics*. Cambridge: Cambridge University Press.

Lewis, O. 1966. *La Vida: A Puerto Rican Family in the Culture of Poverty—San Juan and New York*. New York: Random House.

———. 1975. *Five Families: Case Studies in the Culture of Poverty*. New York: Basic Books.

Lewis, O., with D. Butterworth. 1968. *A Study of Slum Culture: Background for La Vida*. New York: Random House.

Liebow, E. 1967. *Tally's Corner: A Study of Negro Streetcorner Men*. Boston: Little, Brown.

———. 1993. *Tell Them Who I Am: The Lives of Homeless Women*. New York: Free Press.

Linde, C. 1989. "Narrative as a Resource for the Social Constitution of the Self." Paper presented at American Anthropological Society Annual Meeting, November, Washington, D.C.

McDowell, J. H. 1972. "The Mexican Corrido: Formula and Themes in a Ballad Tradition." *Journal of American Folklore* 85: 205–220.

———. 1981. "The Corrido of Greater Mexico as Discourse, Music and Event." In R. Bauman and R. D. Abrahams, eds., *"And Other Neighborly Names": Social Process and Cultural Image in Texas Folklore*, pp. 44–75. Austin: University of Texas Press.

———. 2000. *Poetry and Violence: The Ballad Tradition of Mexico's Costa Chica*. Urbana: University of Illinois Press.

McClelland, D. 1961. *The Achieving Society*. Princeton, N.J.: Van Nostrand.

Marcus, G. E. 1998. *Ethnography through Thick and Thin*. Princeton: Princeton University Press.

Marcus, G. E., and M. J. Fischer. 1986. *Anthropology as Cultural Critique: An Experimental Moment in the Human Sciences*. Chicago: University of Chicago Press.

Marsella, A. J.; G. DeVos; and F. K. Hsu, eds. 1985. *Culture and the Self: Asian and Western Perspectives*. New York: Tavistock Publications.

Martínez, O. J. 1980. *The Chicanos of El Paso: An Assessment of Progress*. Southwestern Studies Monograph no. 59. El Paso: Texas Western Press.

———. 1988. *Troublesome Border*. Tucson: University of Arizona Press.

———. 1994. *Border People: Life and Society in the U.S.-Mexico Borderlands*. Tucson: University of Arizona Press.

Maschio, T. 1994. *To Remember the Faces of the Dead: The Plenitude of Memory in Southwestern New Britain*. Madison: University of Wisconsin Press.

Mead, G. H. 1964. *George Herbert Mead on Social Psychology*. Selected papers, edited and with an introduction by Anselm Strauss. Chicago: University of Chicago Press.

Mendoza, V. T. 1944. *Cincuenta corridos mexicanos*. Mexico City: Ediciones de la Secretaría de Educación Pública.

Mendoza, V. 1964. *Lírica narrativa de México: El corrido*. Mexico City: Universidad Nacional Autónoma de México, Instituto de Investigaciones Estéticas.

Miles, M. B., and A. M. Huberman. 1994. *Qualitative Data Analysis*. 2d ed. Thousand Oaks, Calif.: Sage.

Mirande, A. 1997. *Hombres y Machos: Masculinity and Latino Culture*. Boulder, Colo.: Westview Press.

Moore, M. 2000. "An Anguished Quest for Justice." *Washington Post*, June 26.

Nicolopulos, J. 1997. "The Heroic Corrido: A Premature Obituary?" *Aztlán* 22 (1): 114–138.

Ogbu, J. U. 1990. "Cultural Model, Identity, and Literacy." In J. W. Stigler, R. A. Shweder, and G. Herdt, eds., *Cultural Psychology: Essays on Comparative Human Development*, pp. 520–541. Cambridge: Cambridge University Press.

Paredes, A. 1958. *"With a Pistol in His Hand": A Border Ballad and Its Hero.* Austin: University of Texas Press.

———. 1976. *A Texas-Mexican Cancionero.* Urbana: University of Illinois Press.

———. 1993. *Folklore and Culture on the Texas-Mexican Border.* Edited, with an introduction by R. Bauman. Austin: Center for Mexican American Studies, University of Texas at Austin.

Paz, O. 1985. *The Labyrinth of Solitude and Other Writings.* New York: Grove Press.

Poppa, T. E. 1990. *Drug Lord: The Life and Death of a Mexican Kingpin.* New York: Pharos Books.

Portilla, J. 1966. *La fenomenología del relajo.* Mexico City: Fondo de Cultura Económica.

Quinn, N., and D. Holland. 1987. "Culture and Cognition." In D. Holland and N. Quinn, eds., *Cultural Models of Language and Thought,* pp. 3–40. Cambridge: Cambridge University Press.

Quiñones, S. 1998. "Narco Pop's Bloody Polkas." *Washington Post,* March 1.

———. 2001a. "The Ballad of Chalino Sánchez." In S. Quiñones, *True Tales from Another Mexico.* Albuquerque: University of New Mexico Press.

———. 2001b. "Jesús Malverde." In S. Quiñones, *True Tales from Another Mexico.* Albuquerque: University of New Mexico Press.

———. 2001c. "The Lynch Mob, the Popsicle Kings, Chalino, and the Bronx." In S. Quiñones, *True Tales from Another Mexico.* Albuquerque: University of New Mexico Press.

Ramírez, A. 1990. "Views of the Corrido Hero: Paradigm and Development." *Americas Review* 18 (2): 71–79.

Ramírez-Pimienta, J. C. 1998. "Corrido de narcotráfico en los años ochenta y noventa: Un juicio moral suspendido." *Bilingual Review* 23 (2): 145–156.

Riding, A. 1989. *Distant Neighbors: A Portrait of the Mexicans.* New York: Vintage Books.

Riesman, P. 1992. *First Find Your Child a Good Mother: The Construction of Self in Two African Communities.* New Brunswick: Rutgers University Press.

Riessman, C. K. 1993. *Narrative Analysis.* Qualitative Research Methods Series, vol. 30. Newbury Park, Calif.: Sage.

Rivera, M. 1998. "Sinaloa: El 'orgullo' de ser narco." *La Jornada,* January 4.

Ro, R. 1996. *Gangsta: Merchandising the Rhymes of Violence.* New York: St. Martin's Press.

Rosaldo, R. 1989. *Culture and Truth: The Remaking of Social Analysis.* Boston: Beacon.

Rotella, S. 1998. *Twilight on the Line: Underworlds and Politics at the U.S.-Mexico Border.* New York: Norton.

Said, Edward. 1978. *Orientalism.* New York: Pantheon Books.

Saldívar, J. D. 1986. "Towards a Chicano Poetics: The Making of the Chicano Subject, 1969–1982." *Confluencia* 1 (2): 10–17.

Sanjek, R., ed. 1994. *Anthony Leeds: Cities, Classes, and the Social Order.* Ithaca: Cornell University Press.

Sapir, J. D., and C. Crocker. 1977. *The Social Use of Metaphor.* Philadelphia: University of Pennsylvania Press.

Scott, J. C. 1985. *Weapons of the Weak: Everyday Forms of Peasant Resistance.* New Haven: Yale University Press.

Sklair, L. 1989. *Assembling for Development: The Maquila Industry in Mexico and the United States.* Boston: Unwin Hyman.

Sonnichsen, P. 1975. "Texas-Mexican Border Music." Vols. 2 and 3, *Corridos,* parts 1 and 2, liner notes. Berkeley: Folklyric LP9004.

Sperber, D. 1996. *Explaining Culture: A Naturalistic Approach.* Oxford: Blackwell Publishers.

Spivak, G. 1988. "Can the Subaltern Speak?" In G. Nelson and L. Grossberg, eds., *Marxism and the Interpretation of Culture,* pp. 271–313. Chicago: University of Illinois Press.

Spradley, J. P. 1970. *You Owe Yourself a Drunk: An Ethnography of Urban Nomads.* Boston: Little, Brown.

——. 1972. "Adaptive Strategies of Urban Nomads: The Ethnoscience of Tramp Culture." In T. Weaver and D. White, eds., *The Anthropology of Urban Environments.* Society for Applied Anthropology Monograph Series, no. 11. Washington, D.C.: Society for Applied Anthropology.

Stack, C. 1974. *All Our Kin: Strategies for Survival in a Black Community.* New York: Harper and Row.

Suchlicki, J. 1996. *Mexico: From Montezuma to NAFTA, Chiapas, and Beyond.* Washington, D.C: Brassey's.

Taussig, M. 1993. *Mimesis and Alterity: A Particular History of the Senses.* New York: Routledge.

Thelen, D. 1999. "Mexico's Cultural Landscapes: A Conversation with Carlos Monsiváis." *Journal of American History* 86 (2), Special Issue (September): 613–622.

Thompson, E. P. 1968. *The Making of the English Working Class.* Harmondsworth/Middlesex: Penguin.

Thompson, J. B. 1995. *The Media and Modernity: A Social Theory of the Media.* Stanford: Stanford University Press.

Thrasher, F. M. 1927. *The Gang.* Chicago: University of Chicago Press.

Turner, V. 1967. *The Forest of Symbols: Aspects of Ndembu Ritual.* Ithaca: Cornell University Press.

——. 1974. "Hidalgo: History as Social Drama." In V. Turner, *Dramas, Fields, and Metaphors: Symbolic Action in Human Society,* pp. 98–155. Ithaca: Cornell University Press.

U.S. Census Bureau. 1992. *Current Population Survey.* Washington, D.C.

Valenzuela, José Manuel. 2002. *Jefe de Jefes: Corridos y narcocultura en Mexico.* Mexico: Plaza and Janes.

Wald, E. 1998. "The Ballad of a Mexican Musical Tradition: Corridos Are Still Celebrating Outlaws, Even in the Age of the War on Drugs." *Boston Globe,* January 18, p. K1.

——. 2001. *Narcocorrido: A Journey into the Music of Drugs, Guns, and Guerrillas.* New York: HarperCollins.

Wallerstein, I. 1979. *The Capitalist World Economy*. Cambridge: Cambridge University Press.

Warner, L., and P. S. Lunt. 1947. *The Status System of a Modern Community*. New Haven: Yale University Press.

Warner, L., and L. Srole. 1945. *The Social Systems of American Ethnic Groups*. New Haven: Yale University Press.

Warner, W. L. 1959. *The Living and the Dead: A Study of the Symbolic Life of Americans*. Yankee City Series, vol. 5. New Haven: Yale University Press.

Weber, M. 1994. "Class, Status, and Party." In David B. Grusky, ed., *Social Stratification in Sociological Perspective*, pp. 113–122. Boulder, Colo.: Westview Press.

———. 1958. *The Protestant Ethic and the Spirit of Modern Capitalism*. New York: Charles Scribner's Sons.

Weller, S. C., and A. K. Romney. 1988. *Systematic Data Collection*. Qualitative Research Methods Series, no. 10. Newbury Park, Calif.: Sage.

Wertsch, J. V. 1991. "A Sociocultural Approach to Socially Shared Cognition." In L. B. Resnick, J. M. Levine, and S. D. Teasley, eds., *Socially Shared Cognition*. Washington, D.C.: American Psychological Association.

West, C. 1989. "A Black Culture and Postmodernism." In B. Kruger and P. Mariani, eds., *Remaking History*. Seattle: Bay Press.

———. 1993. *Keeping Faith: Philosophy and Race in America*. New York: Routledge.

Whyte, W. F. 1993 (1943). *Street Corner Society: The Social Structure of an Italian Slum*. 4th ed. Chicago: University of Chicago Press.

Wilson, W. J. 1987. *The Truly Disadvantaged: The Inner City, the Underclass, and Public Policy*. Chicago: University of Chicago Press.

Zavala, I. M. 1992. *Colonialism and Culture: Hispanic Modernisms and the Social Imaginary*. Bloomington: Indiana University Press.

Index